Ancient Egypt for Teens

An Enthralling Guide to Important Events and Rulers in Egyptian History

© Copyright 2025 - All rights reserved.

The content contained within this book may not be reproduced, duplicated, or transmitted without direct written permission from the author or the publisher.

Under no circumstances will any blame or legal responsibility be held against the publisher, or author, for any damages, reparation, or monetary loss due to the information contained within this book, either directly or indirectly.

Legal Notice:

This book is copyright protected. It is only for personal use. You cannot amend, distribute, sell, use, quote, or paraphrase any part, or the content within this book, without the consent of the author or publisher.

Disclaimer Notice:

Please note the information contained within this document is for educational and entertainment purposes only. All effort has been executed to present accurate, up-to-date, reliable, and complete information. No warranties of any kind are declared or implied. Readers acknowledge that the author is not engaging in the rendering of legal, financial, medical, or professional advice. The content within this book has been derived from various sources. Please consult a licensed professional before attempting any techniques outlined in this book.

By reading this document, the reader agrees that under no circumstances is the author responsible for any losses, direct or indirect, that are incurred as a result of the use of the information contained within this document, including, but not limited to, errors, omissions, or inaccuracies.

Free limited time bonus

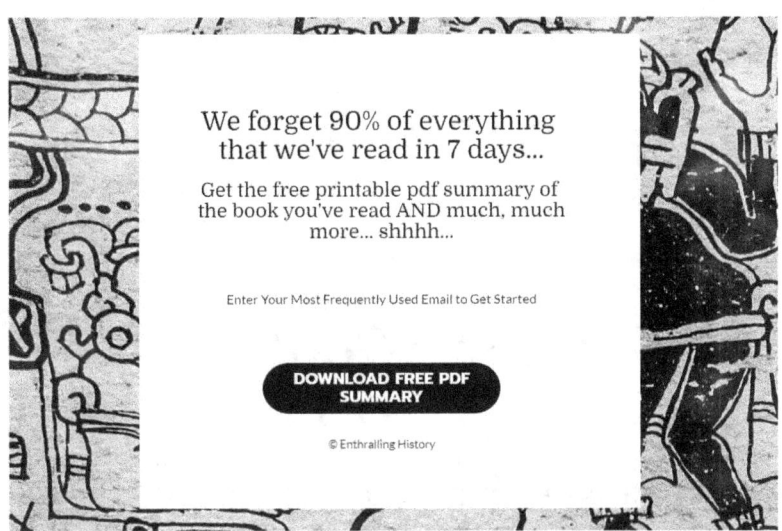

Stop for a moment. We have a free bonus set up for you. The problem is this: we forget 90% of everything that we read after 7 days. Crazy fact, right? Here's the solution: we've created a printable, 1-page pdf summary for this book that you're reading now. All you have to do to get your free pdf summary is to go to the following website: **https://livetolearn.lpages.co/enthrallinghistory/**

Or, Scan the QR code!

Once you do, it will be intuitive. Enjoy, and thank you!

Table of Contents

INTRODUCTION 1
CHAPTER 1: THE RISE OF THE PHARAOHS: EGYPTIAN
UNIFICATION 5
CHAPTER 2: THE MIDDLE KINGDOM AND THE HYKSOS
DYNASTY 17
CHAPTER 3: ANCIENT EGYPTIAN SOCIETY AND CULTURE 29
CHAPTER 4: ANCIENT EGYPTIAN ARCHITECTURE 41
CHAPTER 5: THE AFTERLIFE: EXPLORING LIFE AFTER DEATH
IN ANCIENT EGYPT 52
CHAPTER 6: HATSHEPSUT: THE FEMALE PHARAOH 63
CHAPTER 7: AKHENATEN: THE HERETIC 75
CHAPTER 8: TUTANKHAMUN: A BOY AND HIS LEGACY 85
CHAPTER 9: THE BATTLE OF KADESH 100
CHAPTER 10: THE FALL OF THE NEW KINGDOM 112
ANSWER KEY: ROUNDUP ACTIVITIES 121
HERE'S ANOTHER BOOK BY ENTHRALLING HISTORY THAT
YOU MIGHT LIKE 126
FREE LIMITED TIME BONUS 127
BIBLIOGRAPHY 128
IMAGE SOURCES 131

Introduction

What leaps to mind when thinking of ancient Egypt? Pharaohs? Pyramids? Mummies? All three are essential elements of its history, but there's so much more. This book unpacks the stories of Egypt's pharaohs and ordinary people. What was everyday life like? What was the dark side of the people's relationship with their kings? How did the world's longest river enrich Egypt? Did Egyptian hieroglyphics give birth to the world's first alphabet?

When diving into ancient Egypt's history, the problem of dates arises. What happened when? The ancient Egyptians didn't record dates the same way we do today. Instead, they measured time by the reigns of their kings. For instance, they would write a date like "the third year of Khufu." This leads to another question: when did Khufu reign? It all gets a bit confusing because, sometimes, more than one king ruled part of Egypt at the same time.

Did you know the Egyptians didn't call their kings "pharaohs" until around 1500 BCE in the New Kingdom? The Hebrew people used the title "pharaoh" for Egypt's kings because they wrote the Torah and the rest of the Tanakh (Old Testament) in the New Kingdom or later. The name stuck and is commonly used today, even for earlier kings.

In the third century BCE, an Egyptian priest named Manetho tried to organize ancient Egypt's thousands of years of history. He listed thirty **dynasties**. (A dynasty is when a series of kings and queens from the same family or ethnic group rule). In the 1800s CE, Egyptologists developed the idea of three golden ages: the Old Kingdom, the Middle Kingdom, and the New Kingdom. Egypt had powerful kings, unimaginable wealth, and stunning new technology in these kingdoms. Between these three golden ages, Egypt fell into "intermediate periods." Culture and economics suffered in these times of messy politics.

Scholars fiercely debate the dates for these three kingdoms and their dynasties. The dates in this book are a rough estimation and may be slightly different from other sources. Each of the three kingdoms and intermediate periods had several dynasties. Egypt was occasionally divided so that two or three dynasties ruled simultaneously.

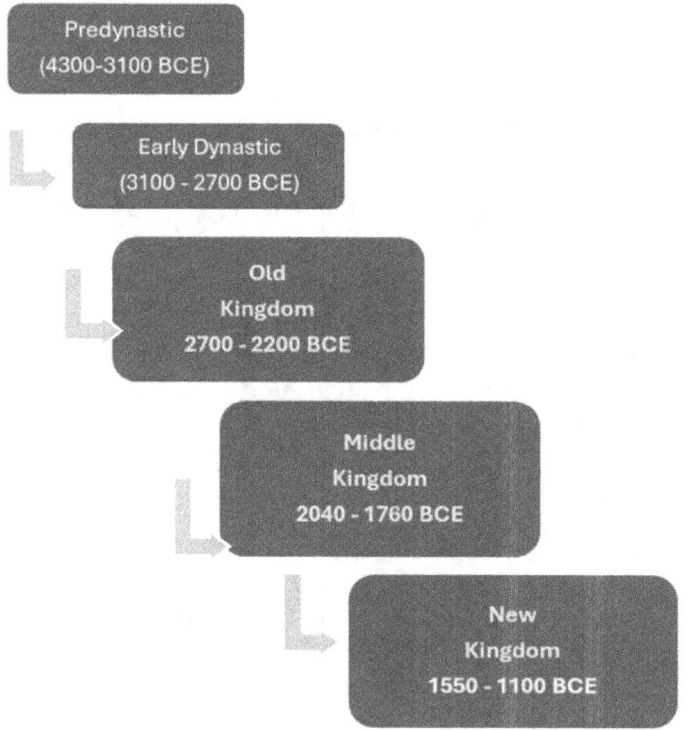

A flowchart of the dynastic periods[1]

This book begins with an overview of Egypt's Predynastic and Early Dynastic eras, when Egypt united and developed its hieroglyphic script. It then delves into the rise of Egypt's great kings who formed the *Old Kingdom*, the Age of the Pyramids. Did you know the Great Pyramid of Giza was the world's tallest structure for almost four millennia? How did they pull off such a fantastic feat 4,600 thousand years ago?

We will then dig into the *Middle Kingdom*, a time of cultural flowering and reunification. One powerful king, Senusret, divided Egypt into three administrative regions. Little did he know that Egypt would split into two (possibly three) separate kingdoms within decades. You'll also learn the answers to the following questions: How did Queen Sobekneferu become Egypt's pharaoh, and what happened when she died without heirs? How did the foreign Hyksos grab power in Egypt? Who were they, and where were they from?

Next, the book explores Egyptian culture. Did the pharaohs really marry their sisters? Why were the ancient Egyptians so consumed with the afterlife? What were the mummies and pyramids all about? How did the Nile River and Egypt's climate affect its culture?

Did you know the Nile River flows **north** from Lake Victoria in Uganda? In ancient times, people called the land Upper Egypt and Lower Egypt. What's confusing is that Upper Egypt is in the south, and Lower Egypt is in the north. However, Upper Egypt is mountainous, and the Nile flows north from these highlands to Lower Egypt, the flat delta region.

Finally, we'll unwrap all the drama of the *New Kingdom* when Egypt pushed its borders north to Syria. What pharaoh turned Egypt's religion upside down? Who was the only god he worshiped? Was the child king, Tutankhamun, physically disabled? How did chariot technology help Ramesses II win the Battle of Kadesh despite being hopelessly outnumbered by the Hittites?

Ancient Egypt's story has intriguing twists and turns that will keep you turning the pages. But aside from being entertaining, what's the point of reading history? History unlocks secrets from the past, shedding light on why the world is the way it is today. History is all about change and how and why it happens. It inspires us to be agents of change for a better future. As we read the history of Ancient Egypt, we'll see how it passed through multiple transformations that sparked innovative technology and culture. On the other hand, the dark side of Egypt's history is a lesson in what *not* to do.

Now, let's jump back in time on a journey through ancient Egypt's spellbinding history.

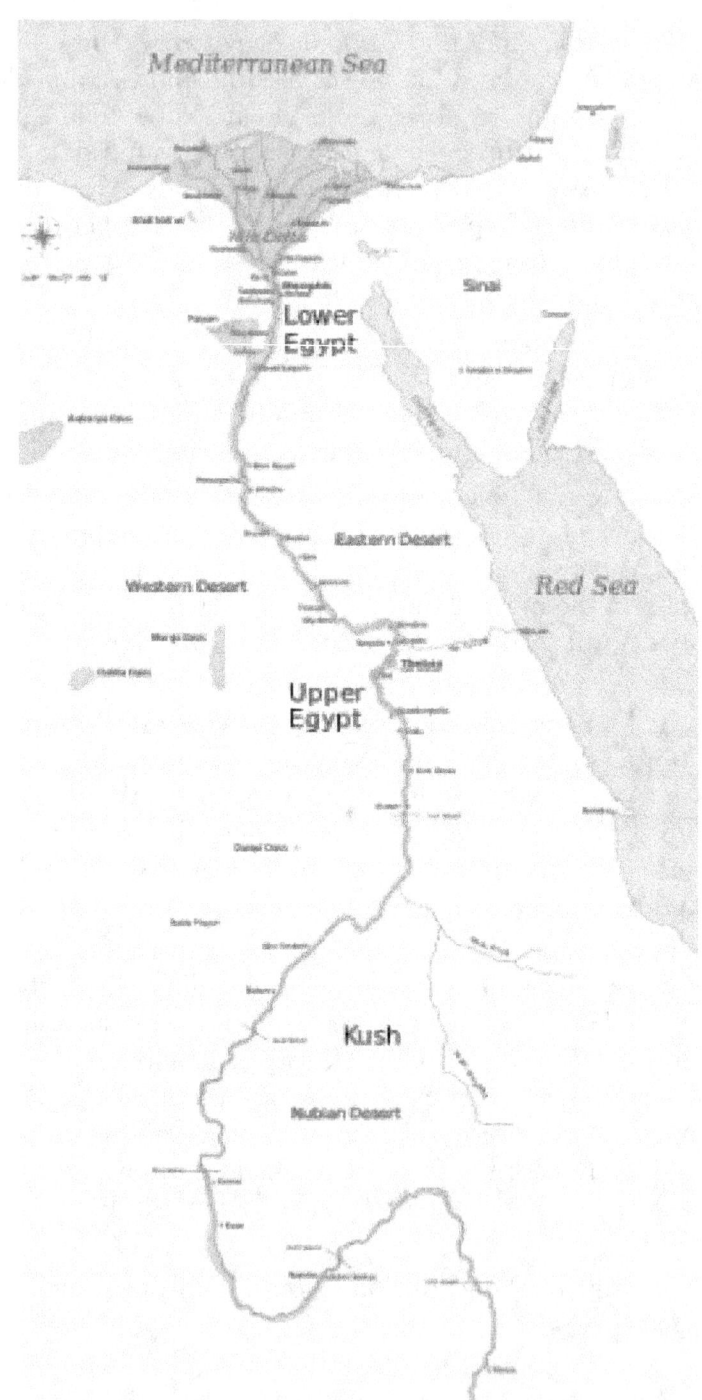

Upper and Lower Egypt

Chapter 1: The Rise of the Pharaohs: Egyptian Unification

King Djoser was in the depths of despair. The rain had stopped for seven years. Unimaginable suffering gripped Egypt. Children were wailing in hunger. No one seemed to know how to make it rain again. Djoser called for his advisor, Imhotep, an architect and priest of the sun god Ra.

"What should I do?" he asked Imhotep. "Who is the god of the Nile's headwaters? We need to ask him for help!"

"Let me travel upstream and find out," Imhotep said.

Imhotep returned to report, "I found a temple called Joy-of-Life. Khnum is its god. He opens and shuts the gates of the Nile."

Djoser made an offering of beer and oxen to Khnum. That night, Khnum visited Djoser in a dream.

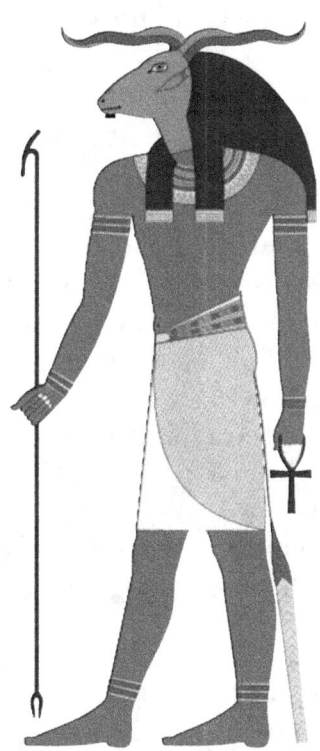

The ram-headed god Khnum[8]

"My temple on the island of Elephantine is falling down. I gave the Egyptians life through my river! Now, everyone has lost respect for me."

When he awoke, Djoser ordered the temple to be torn down. He built a beautiful new temple on its foundations. The famine ended, to everyone's relief.

The ruins of that temple to Khnum are still on Elephantine Island, 4,700 years later. The stone stela with this story was found on Seheil Island in the Nile, just south of Elephantine Island.

Predynastic Egypt (4300–3100 BCE)

Djoser was the first king of Egypt's Old Kingdom, but what happened before that? How did Egypt's early people live in the misty ages before they started to write? Archaeological evidence shows that in Predynastic Egypt, people built oval huts with mud-plastered walls and woven mats on the floor. They herded cattle, sheep, and goats and grew wheat and barley. They ground the grain into flour and formed a round, flat dough. Then they lit a fire inside a dome-shaped clay oven and let it burn until the walls got hot. After putting out the fire, they slapped the bread dough on the inside of the oven's walls, which baked the bread.

By 3400 BCE, ancient Egyptians were building houses from sunbaked bricks. Some homes were grander, with central courtyards. Egypt's early cities sprang up in the delta region. Xois was built, and people continually lived there for almost 3,800 years. Nekhen (Hierakonpolis) grew into a town of 5,000 people by 3400 BCE.

What about mummification? When did that start? Egyptians usually buried their dead in desert cemeteries, where the hot sand would naturally dry out and mummify the bodies. By 3350 BCE, Egyptians started wrapping their dead in linen cloth soaked in embalming agents like aromatic plant extract, gum, natural petroleum, and pine resin. By 3200 BCE, they began building large brick or limestone tombs with multiple rooms for burying family members.

Between 3400 and 3200 BCE, Egyptians began drawing pictographs in Abydos. These were simple pictures that could represent either the object in the image or another word with a similar sound as the object. These pictographs evolved into hieroglyphic writing. In the earliest stages of hieroglyphics, Egyptians didn't write sentences. They used the pictographs for labels and record keeping.

Pictographs from Abydos[4]

Archaeological digs from this era show the Egyptians had brilliant blue beads made from the lapis lazuli stone. Yet, Egypt didn't have lapis lazuli, so where did it come from? The nearest source was Afghanistan, over 2,000 miles away! Southern Iraq was probably the middleman in long-distance trade, as Iraq's Ubaid culture had the same beads.

The Ubaid traded with both Egypt and Afghanistan in long and arduous journeys by donkey over the deserts. The humble donkey was the world's first transportation animal, domesticated from the wild African ass around 5000 BCE.

Other items made from lapis lazuli were cylinder seals. Egypt adopted these from southern Iraq around 3300 BCE. A cylinder seal was a stone cylinder about four inches long with carvings of tiny pictures on it. When the owner rolled it in soft clay, it left an impression of the image. The clay hardened, and the picture represented the owner's signature.

Egypt Unites! Early Dynastic Egypt (3100–2700 BCE)

Over the next four centuries, there was an explosion of culture as writing and stunning technological advances developed. For the first time, Upper and Lower Egypt united into one country. How did that happen? It was the work of Narmer, the first king of Egypt's unified state. With a central government and economy, Egypt could organize massive projects like building pyramids. This didn't happen until the Old Kingdom emerged, but Egypt's Early Dynastic era set the stage.

Drawing of the Narmer Palette[5]

"Stinging Catfish"

What do we know about Narmer, the first king of unified Egypt? The hieroglyphs for Narmer's name are the signs for "catfish" and "painful." The dates are fuzzy, but he ruled around 3100 BCE. He was probably Menes, a king mentioned by the historian Manetho. Egyptian kings had personal names and throne names, which can get confusing. Narmer, the "Stinging Catfish," unified Egypt and began its First Dynasty. Narmer was from Upper Egypt and conquered Lower Egypt, which was epic since Lower Egypt had developed earlier and was more powerful. Upper Egypt now had the upper hand.

The "Narmer Palette" is a two-foot-high stone slab. On carvings on one side, Narmer brandishes a mace, a club-like weapon. He grabs a kneeling captive by the hair, probably Lower Egypt's ruler. A falcon represents Horus, the king-making god. On the opposite side of the palette are two "serpopards," leopards with serpent necks. Their intertwining necks represent Upper and Lower Egypt's union.

Drawing of serpopards from the Narber Palette[6]

Narmer expanded Egypt's power into the Sinai Peninsula and Canaan (ancient Israel and Palestine). Artifacts found in Gaza and Israel have his name on them. His long reign ended when a hippopotamus killed him. (Yes, hippos are deadly animals. They kill about 500 people every year in Africa!)

Narmer's wife was the powerful Queen Neithhotep. Their son, Hor-Aha, was still a small child when Narmer died. Queen Neithhotep ruled Egypt until her son grew up and became the next king.

The MacGregor Plaque is an ivory tablet dating to about 2985 BCE from the tomb of King Den. In the writing on the tablet, Den boasts of making "the first strike to the east." What does he mean by "east?" Narmer had already pressed east as far as Canaan. Did he mean Mesopotamia (ancient Iraq)? We can't be sure, but the picture on the tablet shows him grasping the hair of an eastern king who wears his hair and beard braided in Mesopotamian style.

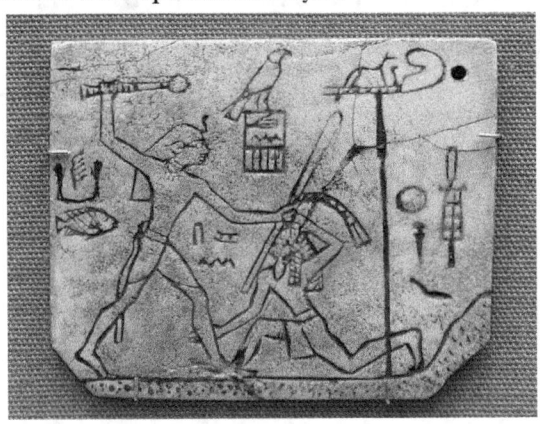

King Den and his eastern captive[7]

The Old Kingdom: Age of the Pyramids (2700–2200 BCE)

After four centuries and two dynasties, a new era dawned for Egypt. The Old Kingdom was the first of Egypt's three golden ages. This age began when the first pyramid rose from the sand to dominate Egypt's landscape. The energy, manpower, and materials poured into building the pyramids in this era are mind-blowing. Dynasties three through six ruled Egypt in these glory days.

Djoser

As we said earlier, King Djoser began the Old Kingdom, the era of pyramids. He built the first pyramid and was the first king of the Third Dynasty. Ornate architecture blossomed under his reign. He extended Egypt past Libya's borders and took back the Sinai Peninsula, a valuable source of turquoise and copper. Upper and Lower Egypt had separated in the turmoil toward the end of the Early Dynastic period, but Djoser or his father brought the two back together. No sooner did Djoser become king than he jumped into multiple building projects like nothing ever seen before.

Mastabas: Pyramid Precursors

Before Djoser, Egyptian royals were buried in mastaba tombs, which had flat roofs and mudbrick walls that sloped in. A mastaba was rectangular and about twenty to thirty feet high. The dead person wasn't buried inside the mastaba but under it. A shaft went underground to a small burial room; another shaft descended to a second room next to the burial room. This room held things the dead person needed in the afterlife, like beer, clothing, food, and jewelry.

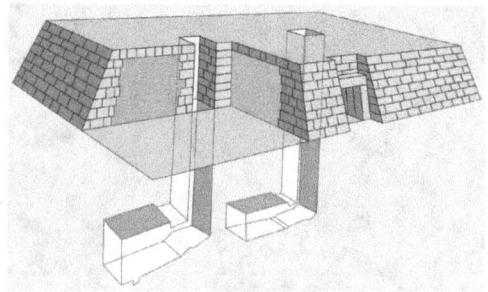

A mastaba[*]

The First Pyramid

Djoser had his tomb built like a mastaba, but instead of one layer, he wanted six layers. His architect, Imhotep, built each layer slightly smaller than the one underneath, forming steps. Instead of mud bricks, he used stone. The Step Pyramid of Djoser soared 204 feet high, the highest structure in the world up to that time. The Sumerians in ancient Iraq had been building ziggurats, similar to step pyramids, but none were yet this high.

Djoser's actual burial place was under the pyramid, as in the mastabas. His burial shaft descended ninety feet under the pyramid. Imhotep discouraged tomb robbers by building a maze of tunnels so that finding the royal burial vault was nearly impossible. Despite Imhotep's best efforts, ancient tomb robbers broke into Djoser's tomb and stole almost everything. All that was left was a mummified left foot.

Egypt's first pyramid, the Step Pyramid of Djoser°

After Djoser's reign, most of Egypt's Old Kingdom rulers were obsessed with building pyramids. An astonishing amount of their attention and planning revolved around their eventual resting place. As the pyramids grew larger and more elaborate, they needed a monumental and knowledgeable workforce to erect them. This activity required a strong central government, which the Old Kingdom had most of the time.

Thousands of workers cut the stones at a quarry and transported them to the building sites. But Egypt didn't have the wheel until the Fifth Dynasty, so how did they move those hefty stones over long distances? They used gigantic sleds pulled through the sand. Workers ahead of the sled poured water on the sand, making it slippery. Most pyramids were near today's Cairo, stretching about forty miles along the Nile.

The First "True" Pyramids

The step pyramids were the "steppingstones" to the first "real" pyramids with smooth sides and a pointed top. King Sneferu of the Fourth Dynasty built the first three smooth-sided, pointy-top pyramids around 2500 BCE. His first pyramid was a disaster. The architects only used a rock foundation for the inner core. The outer layers lay on a sand foundation, which couldn't support the pyramid's weight. The pyramid collapsed in the final stage of construction, burying the workers underneath it.

Sneferu didn't give up. He built a pyramid at Dahshur. However, his architects were still figuring out how to get the angles of a true pyramid right. They erected the pyramid at a 55-degree angle, which worked fine until they were about halfway to the top. The pyramid began showing instability, so the builders switched to a flatter 43-degree angle. This made the Bent Pyramid appear bent at the top, hence the name. Dissatisfied, the architects immediately built the Red Pyramid entirely at a 43-degree angle. Its stones were a rusty red.

The Bent Pyramid[10]

Khufu, Builder of the Great Pyramid

Khufu was the next pharaoh after Sneferu and probably his son. He was remembered as an oppressive king who did not value the lives of his people. He pressed the Egyptians into forced labor to build his masterpiece, the world's highest pyramid of all time. Standing at about 481 feet high, the Great Pyramid was the highest building in the world for almost 4,000 years. It was also the largest pyramid until the Mesoamericans built the Cholula Pyramid in Mexico, beginning in the third century BCE. The Cholula Pyramid had a much larger base and volume, but the Great Pyramid was still higher.

The Westcar Papyrus, written in the seventeenth century BCE, tells five stories about magical happenings. The first story deals with a miracle performed by Imhotep during Djoser's reign. Khufu's son, Khafre, supposedly tells the second story, which happened in the earlier reign of King Nebka. According to the story, the king's chief priest discovered his wife was cheating on him. Her lover was sneaking into the priest's property to meet with her. To get revenge, the priest made a wax crocodile and used his magic to bring it to life. His servant threw it into the stream that his wife's lover crossed to visit her. The crocodile grabbed the man, pulled him to the bottom for seven days, then ate him.

Khufu's son, Baufra, tells the third story about his grandfather, King Sneferu. One day, the king was bored and had nothing to do, so he had twenty beautiful young women row him around the palace lake. One of the young ladies wore a necklace with a fish ornament, her favorite jewelry piece. When the necklace fell into the lake, she was hysterical.

"Don't worry. You can have any necklace in my treasury!" Sneferu said, trying to console her.

But the young woman only wanted her necklace at the bottom of the lake. Finally, the king's priest split the water so she could get her necklace, then returned the water to where it had been.

Khufu's son Hordjedef tells the fourth story about a magician named Dedi who claimed he could tame lions and reattach an animal's head that had been cut off. He also knew how many secret rooms were in the shrine of Thoth. Khufu called him to his court to test him out. "Here's a criminal," Khufu said. "We'll cut his head off, and you can put it back on."

"No. We can't kill a man. That isn't proper for dark magic. Bring some animals instead."

Khufu had his servants cut off the heads of a goose, a duck, and a bull. The magician successfully reattached them.

"Well done!" said Khufu. "Now, tell me, how many rooms are in the shrine of Thoth."

"I don't actually know," Dedi admitted. "But I do know *where* they are. However, I can't tell you how to get into the rooms. The gods haven't given you access. The future king born from the woman Rededjet, wife of the priest of Ra, will have access to the rooms of the shrine."

The child of the priest and Rededjet who became a king was Userkaf, the first king of the Fifth Dynasty.

Dedi tells the fifth story, giving a prophecy about Rededjet and her triplets. The birth was dangerous, so the god Ra sent Isis and other deities to assist her. The three boys were safely delivered and came out of their mother with lapis lazuli crowns and gold covering their arms and legs.

The Old Kingdom Crumbles

The Egyptians' preoccupation with building pyramids led to the priests acquiring more power. Everyone was so consumed with the afterlife that they let the priests control things. They carried out the rituals for the dead and started calling the shots in Egypt. During the Fifth and Sixth dynasties, the kings gradually became weaker and more irrelevant. The solid central government began to melt away, and the cost of building elaborate pyramids bankrupted the country. Priests and **nomarchs** (governors) held dominance over local areas.

A horrendous drought and famine in the Sixth Dynasty devastated Egypt. The **4.2-kiloyear BP** event was one of human history's worst climate changes. (**Kiloyear** means a thousand years, and **BP** means "before present," so it happened about 4,200 years before the twentieth century CE.) It struck the Middle East, bringing cooler temperatures and only half the average rainfall. Drought, political woes, and financial disaster led to the fall of the Old Kingdom.

In the First Intermediate Period (2200–2040 BCE), each region of Egypt ruled itself. The Seventh through Tenth dynasties ruled this era, but not over the entire country. In these chaotic times, miscreants raided tombs, destroyed precious artwork, and broke up the statues of the earlier kings.

Roundup Activity: Who Am I?

Match the person with who they were or what they did. Check your answers in the back of the book.

1. Dedi — I was the first king of a unified Egypt. A hippo killed me.

2. Djoser — I was King Narmer's wife. After he died, I ruled Egypt until my son grew up.

3. Imhotep — I built Egypt's first pyramid and rescued Egypt from a famine.

4. Khnum — I was the god of the Nile's headwaters. I got angry when my temple fell into disrepair.

5. Khufu — I was Djoser's right-hand man. I was also an architect and priest of the sun god Ra.

6. Narmer — I was a Fourth Dynasty king who built three pyramids until I finally got it right.

7. Queen Neithhotep — I built Egypt's Great Pyramid, the highest in the world.

8. Rededjet — I was a magician who could reattach an animal's head that had been cut off.

9. Sneferu — I gave birth to triplets. One baby was Userkaf, the first king of the Fifth Dynasty.

Chapter 2: The Middle Kingdom and the Hyksos Dynasty

Egypt's Second Golden Age: The Middle Kingdom (2040-1760 BCE)

How was order restored to Egypt? Several cities were fighting for control of the country. The two strongest were Thebes in the south and Herakleopolis in the north. King Mentuhotep II of Thebes trounced Hierakonpolis, becoming the Middle Kingdom's first king. Once again, Egypt was united. It was a time of spectacular strides in culture. New painting and sculpture techniques in this golden age influenced the rest of Egypt's ancient history. The stability brought by powerful kings allowed trade to soar, enriching Egypt.

Mentuhotep's son and grandson ruled Egypt for several decades. Then, Amenemhat I came on the scene. He was King Mentuhotep IV's advisor and not from a royal family, yet he thought he could do a better job running Egypt. Somehow, he stole the throne

Mentuhotep II, the first king of the Middle Kingdom[11]

for himself. He moved Egypt's capital from Thebes to Iti-tawi, further south. Amenemhat I began Egypt's Twelfth Dynasty, which ruled Egypt for two centuries. This dynasty took Egypt to a peak of wealth and culture.

The Asian Invasion

People from *West Asia* or the *Levant* (Syria, Lebanon, and Canaan) had been moving to Egypt since the First Intermediate Period. What brought them to Egypt? Often, it was a lack of rain. The biblical book of Genesis says that a famine brought Abraham from Canaan to Egypt. He lived there briefly but fell out of favor with the Egyptian king over his wife, Sarah, who was also his half-sister. He ended up getting kicked out of Egypt. Like Abraham, other shepherds needed grass and fresh water for their sheep, cattle, and camels.

Egypt was friendly with Syria as far back as the Old Kingdom. The Syrian king Irkab-Damu of Ebla received gifts from Egypt's king. When he died around 2340 BCE, the gifts were buried with him in his tomb. Egypt had a trade colony in the coastal city of Byblos, Lebanon. Ships traveled back and forth from Byblos to Egypt in a thriving trade.

The Egyptians called the people from Syria, Lebanon, and Canaan "Aamu," which meant "*West Asians*."

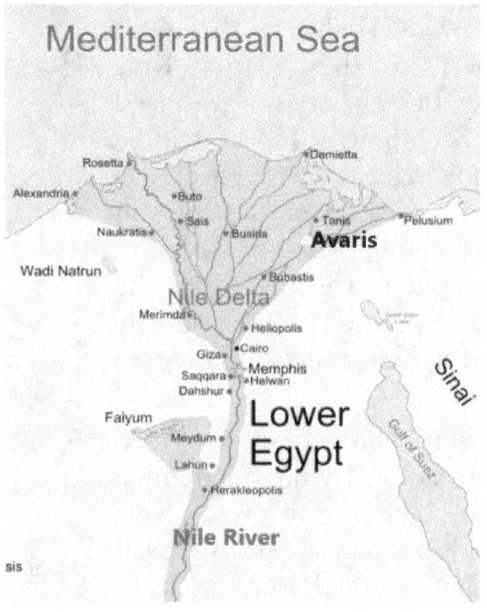

Avaris on the eastern Nile Delta[13]

Most West Asians who came to Egypt lived in the Nile Delta, where the Nile split into seven branches that spread out for 150 miles and emptied into the Mediterranean Sea. Egypt's Nile Delta usually remained relatively green even during a drought because the Nile's seven branches flooded yearly. This lush region of Egypt was great for the shepherds' flocks.

Many West Asians lived in Avaris, a city on the easternmost branch of the Nile close to the Mediterranean Sea. It was a key trade city with Byblos in Lebanon. Scientists did an isotope analysis of the skeletons buried in Avaris's cemeteries. Curiously, they found that 77 percent of the non-Egyptians were female. Why? Maybe women were brought in as enslaved people or wives. The Amorite women of Syria and Canaan were famous weavers.

The Phoenicians of Lebanon were the masters of the sea. Egypt imported Phoenician shipbuilders and sailors to build ships and sail Egyptian fleets. Cattle breeders, weavers, stone masons, artisans, and military men also found a warm welcome in Egypt. These migrants got new Egyptian names when they arrived but also kept their West Asian names. Some West Asians rose through the ranks to become governors or the pharaoh's advisors.

The book of Genesis says that Abraham's grandson Israel (Jacob) brought his clan of seventy people to live in Egypt. They joined his son Joseph in Egypt during a famine. Joseph was enslaved in Egypt until the king elevated him to second in command.

Based on the biblical timeline, Israel's family came to Egypt in the Middle Kingdom. A powerful governor named Khnumhotep II ruled Egypt's Oryx *nome* (province). His elaborate tomb has a painting of a family arriving from Canaan. The date on the painting is the sixth year of King Senusret II. It must have been an event of some importance to be painted on his tomb with a date.

A family from Canaan arrives with gifts for the Egyptian king.[18]

The Alphabet's Ancestor

Around 3,500 years ago, someone carved graffiti on a rock in the Sinai Peninsula near an Egyptian turquoise mine. When scholars found it in the early 1900s CE, they got excited. The writing was a form of Egyptian hieroglyphics. However, its words were in a Semitic language (spoken by West Asians), not Egyptian. The writer knew how to write Egyptian hieroglyphics but applied it to his own language. Scholars called this new form of writing "Proto-Sinaitic." It gave birth to the Phoenician alphabet of Lebanon.

Word	Proto-Sinaitic	Phoenician	Latin
'alp ("ox")	(ox head)	(tilted K)	A
mem ("water")	(wavy line)	(zigzag)	M
'en ("eye")	(eye)	(circle)	O

Proto-Sinaitic, Phoenician, and Latin alphabets compared[14]

"Beautiful Crocodile," Egypt's First Woman Pharaoh (1764–1760 BCE)

Sobekneferu stood at the deathbed of her half-brother and husband, Amenemhat IV. Who would rule Egypt now? They both came from a long line of strong and stable kings of Egypt. Sobekneferu's mother was the queen and official wife of their father, Amenemhat III. But Amenemhat IV's mother was a minor wife and not royalty. The only way to get the Egyptians to accept him as king was for Amenemhat IV to marry Sobekneferu. (Yes, Egyptian royalty commonly married their siblings to keep the sacred royal blood in the family.)

Amenemhat IV only reigned for nine years and then died without any children by his sister Sobekneferu. His minor wife huddled weeping in the corner with her two small sons. Sobekneferu glanced at them. The boys wouldn't be old enough to rule for years, and they weren't legitimate. They weren't born to a royal wife, nor was their father. There was only one thing to do. She would have to be the next pharaoh. Sobekneferu, whose name meant "Beautiful Crocodile," became Egypt's first woman pharaoh. Other women had ruled Egypt as regents while their sons grew up. However, Sobekneferu was the first woman ruler of Egypt who wasn't a regent. She had full royal titles.

During the reigns of Amenemhat IV and Sobekneferu, the West Asians were stirring up trouble in northeastern Egypt. They blocked the roads to the Sinai Peninsula. Egypt had turquoise and copper mines in the Sinai; now, they couldn't get to them.

Sobekneferu only ruled for about four years and died around 1760 BCE. Sobekneferu had no children, so she was the last pharaoh of Egypt's Twelfth Dynasty. The Middle Kingdom ended with her death around 1760 BCE.

The Chaotic Second Intermediate Period

A wobbly Thirteenth Dynasty continued to rule from Iti-tawi. These kings didn't control all of Egypt, just Upper Egypt. Few kings ruled for more than three years; some only ruled for a few months before a contender overthrew them. The first two kings were probably the sons of Amenemhat IV's non-royal wife. In these tumultuous times, royal blood had lost its importance. Most of the kings of this dynasty were not from royal families and were proud of it. The Thirteenth Dynasty struggled along for about 150 years.

Egypt's First Foreign Kings

Meanwhile, a rival Fourteenth Dynasty ruled the Nile Delta region. Its rulers were foreigners, but not the same West Asians as the Hyksos Fifteenth Dynasty. Who were they? They may have been Canaanites, as they had a warm trade relationship with Canaan. The kings of this dynasty didn't keep many written records, so we have to piece together what the archaeological record reveals.

The Fourteenth Dynasty ruled northeastern Egypt. At first, they fought the Thirteenth Dynasty in southern Egypt, but eventually, the two dynasties decided they needed to cooperate to survive. So, they formed a truce and traded with each other. The Fourteenth Dynasty allowed the folks in the Thirteenth Dynasty to sail up the Nile to the Mediterranean Sea. The Thirteenth Dynasty let the Fourteenth Dynasty people pass through their land to reach Nubia in the south. Unlike the Thirteenth Dynasty rulers, the Fourteenth Dynasty kings had long and stable reigns.

Another deadly famine rocked Egypt around 1700 BCE. The suffering was worse in the south, as the branches of the Nile provided irrigation for farms and herds in the north. But this drought lasted for fifty years. It eventually took its toll on the northern Fourteenth Dynasty, especially after an epidemic struck. People buried their dead in mass graves. Kings only ruled for months before they died of starvation, disease, or assassination.

The Hyksos Dynasty

Hyksos is Greek for the Egyptian word *Heka Khasut*, which means "foreign kings" or "shepherd kings." At first, the title seemed to be a generic catch-all phrase for foreign chieftains. It didn't mean a specific group of people. The Twelfth Dynasty governor Khnumhotep's tomb painting shows a man leading an ibex. The tomb inscription said he was "Abisha the Hyksos."

Abisha the Hyksos[15]

Later, the Egyptians used "Hyksos" for the West Asians that ruled Egypt's Fifteenth Dynasty. Their culture points to them being from Syria or Lebanon. The Egyptian historian Manetho said they were Phoenicians. Most likely, they were Amorites from the port city of Byblos in Lebanon. Avaris always had a warm relationship with Byblos, which the Amorites conquered in 2150 BCE.

The Hyksos did not leave any records telling how they conquered Egypt. The Egyptians' story was that the gods were angry at the Egyptians. Before the Egyptians knew what was happening, a swarm of foreigners had swept into Egypt from the east, catching the Egyptians by surprise. The crude foreigners burned down Egypt's cities, flattened its temples, and enslaved the people.

However, archaeologist Manfred Bietak, who spent decades unearthing the ruins of Avaris, says archaeology tells a different story. He says the Hyksos were in Egypt all along. Some lived in Avaris with the other West Asians; others lived throughout Egypt. They took advantage of the turmoil caused by the previously mentioned famine and epidemic. Over half of Egypt's population had died, destabilizing the Thirteenth Dynasty in the north and the Fourteenth Dynasty in the south.

Around 1650 BCE, the Hyksos conquered Memphis, making it the first capital of the new Fifteenth Dynasty. They elected their first king, Salatis. The Hyksos swiftly conquered the rest of Egypt and forced Upper and Lower Egypt to pay *tribute* (something like a tax). Salatis was concerned that the Assyrians of northern Iraq might invade, so he built fortresses along Egypt's northeastern border. He also stationed 240,000 troops there.

Salatis decided that Avaris would be a better capital as it was near the border and the Mediterranean Sea. Avaris grew to about 25,000 people, becoming Egypt's largest city of its day. The Egyptian king Kamose later described Avaris's busy and prosperous harbor. It had hundreds of ships filled with gold, silver, bronze axes, lapis lazuli, turquoise, incense, and expensive wood.

Around 1640 BCE, the Egyptians regrouped and formed an opposing kingdom, the Sixteenth Dynasty. The native Egyptians' capital was Thebes. At first, the Hyksos Fifteenth Dynasty and the Egyptian Sixteenth Dynasty were hostile. But they eventually became friendly, traded with each other, and permitted passage through their sections of the Nile. Around 1580 BCE, the Seventeenth Dynasty replaced the

Sixteenth Dynasty at Thebes. Within decades, this dynasty grew strong enough to challenge the Hyksos.

Noisy Hippos

The humorous and probably fictional story, "The Quarrel of Apophis and Seqenenre," represents the growing tension between the Hyksos king Apepi (Apophis) and the Seventeenth Dynasty king Seqenenre. The Egyptian king was irritated that he had to pay tribute to Apepi. He found it appalling that Apepi spent so much time worshiping the god Seth (Baal) but ignored the other Egyptian gods. Meanwhile, Apepi was looking for a way to annoy Seqenenre even further. He wanted to test out the strength of Seqenenre's god, Amun-Ra.

Apepi called in his advisors and picked their brains.

"Hippos! Test him with hippos, O sovereign lord."

"Hippos?"

A hippo figurine from Egypt's late Middle Kingdom[16]

"Yes. Demand that Seqenenre remove the hippopotamuses from that canal outside Thebes. Tell him they're keeping us awake with their roaring."

Apepi snorted with laughter. Thebes was about 480 miles south of Avaris. No one in Avaris was hearing hippos at Thebes. Yet, he sent his ambassador to deliver the message to Seqenenre. At first, the Egyptian king sat in a stunned silence. Then he gathered his wits.

"Where are my manners? You must be starving! Here, have some of this delicious beef. And try this cake! Now, go back and tell Apepi I'll take care of the hippos."

As soon as the ambassador left, Seqenenre called his advisors. What should they do? No one could come up with an answer. But Apepi wasn't done goading Seqenenre. He called his ambassador to send another message.

At this juncture in the story, the ancient papyrus on which it was written is broken off. We don't find out what happened to the noisy hippos or who won the battle of wits. However, Thebes grew in strength and stopped paying tribute to Avaris. It even blocked the Hyksos trade routes to Nubia in the south. The two kings eventually warred against each other, and the Hyksos won. Seqenenre died a horrible death with multiple axe wounds to his face.

Ahmose Defeats the Hyksos

Seqenenre's son Kamose became king in his late teens, the last ruler of the Seventeenth Dynasty. Neither the Egyptians nor the Hyksos wanted to prolong the war. However, Kamose thought his war council was dropping the ball. He couldn't let the Hyksos get away with killing his father. And he was indignant that Thebes had to pay tribute to Avaris. Moreover, the Hyksos were blocking Egyptian ships from sailing up the Nile and into the Mediterranean.

"I'll take Apepi on, that Syrian prince with weak arms! I'll rip open his belly!" Kamose raged in his inscriptions.

He sailed his navy downstream to Avaris. "Look! I'm here! Everything you own is mine now! Is your heart stopping, you vile West Asian?"

Kamose raided the harbor and sank its ships but could not breach Avaris's high walls. However, he bragged about not losing a single man. Of course, he apparently didn't engage anyone in battle, so the Hyksos probably didn't lose any men either. At this point, Kamose made his younger brother Ahmose a co-ruler with him, although he was only ten.

Kamose then marched south to fight the Nubians and died while still in his twenties.

Ahmose I came to the throne around 1550 BCE. His reign began Egypt's New Kingdom and its Eighteenth Dynasty. The war with the Hyksos paused until Ahmose grew up. In the meantime, his mother, Ahhotep, ruled Egypt as regent. Earlier, Kamose had captured some horses and chariots from the Hyksos. Ahmose used these as prototypes to build his own chariots to fight the Hyksos. This was the first time Egyptians used war chariots.

Pharaoh Ahmose defeats a Hyksos warrior. [17]

Ahmose defeated the Hyksos once and for all in his nineteenth year as king. One of the Egyptian commanders, whose name was also Ahmose, wrote an eyewitness account of the Egyptians chasing the Hyksos out of Egypt. He said they ran to the city of Sharuhen in Canaan.

When the Egyptians tracked them down, they fought for three years. Finally, the Hyksos abandoned Sharuhen and ran to Syria. At this point, King Ahmose returned to Egypt, probably to avoid fight the Hyksos's allies in Syria.

The Hyksos Legacy

The Hyksos brought new war technology, enabling Egypt to dominate its neighbors in the New Kingdom. The Hyksos also introduced the first horses to Egypt. (The Egyptians hadn't even use animal-pulled carts until the Thirteenth Dynasty.) The Hyksos' spoke-wheeled chariots were fast and could turn on a dime.

The Egyptians had been using a simple bow from one piece of wood. The Hyksos brought the superior rounded composite bow to Egypt. This bow has several pieces glued together, making it more flexible. Arrows shot from a composite bow fly faster and farther and are more deadly.

The West Asian man on the left carries a composite bow and a duckbilled axe. The man on the right is playing a box lyre.[18]

Roundup Activity: What Happened When?

Look at the key events in ancient Egypt's Middle Kingdom and Second Intermediate Period. Number them (to the right of each sentence) in the order they happened. Check your answers in the back of the book.

1. Ahmose begins the New Kingdom and the Eighteenth Dynasty.
2. Ahmose conquered the Hyksos once and for all.
3. Amenemhat I usurped the throne and started the Twelfth Dynasty.
4. Mentuhotep II united Egypt again, beginning the Middle Kingdom.
5. Seqenenre was killed, and Kamose became king.
6. Sobekneferu, the "Beautiful Crocodile," died.
7. The Egyptians regrouped and formed the Sixteenth Dynasty.
8. The Hyksos conquered Memphis.
9. The Seventeenth Dynasty replaced the Sixteenth Dynasty at Thebes.

Chapter 3: Ancient Egyptian Society and Culture

In this chapter, we'll examine the daily lives of ordinary Egyptians. What kind of food did they eat? What was their clothing like? What was their religion, and how did they practice it? What was unique about Egyptian art? Why was the Nile more than just a river? And why did the Egyptians use a beetle-shaped seal to sign their names? Let's uncover the answers to these questions and more.

What Did the Ancient Egyptians Eat and Wear?

The ancient Egyptian's favorite drink was beer. They drank it every day. But Egyptian beer wasn't like our beer today. It was thick, like a milkshake, and they even used long straws to drink it. Beer was stored and served in jars with a narrow neck. The Egyptians made their beer by first baking bread dough made from emmer wheat until it was gooey in the middle. They crumbled the bread, mixed it with water, and let it sit. The yeast in the bread caused it to ferment. Even today, Egyptians drink home-brewed *bouza*, which is remarkably close to the ancient beer.

The main food in everyday Egyptian meals was barley or emmer wheat bread. Egyptians enjoyed vegetable side dishes like green onions, cucumber, celery, and lettuce. They loved fruit like melons, dates, figs, and grapes. The usual protein was stewed lentils, chickpeas, or beans. They also made cheese and ate eggs and fish. Meat was usually only eaten on special occasions. At weddings, festivals, and other special days,

Egyptians typically ate duck, geese, beef, mutton, and pork. Some of their stranger delicacies included mice and hedgehogs!

A West Asian man, apparently married to an Egyptian woman, drinks beer from a straw.[19]

Upper Egypt includes a section of the Sahara Desert, one of the world's hottest and dryest places. All of Egypt is hot, with an average summer temperature of 95 degrees Fahrenheit (35 degrees Celsius). Egyptian children under six usually wore nothing except anklets and bracelets. Workers and enslaved people sometimes wore nothing but a thong. Whether royal or ordinary, men usually only wore a lightweight, wraparound "kilt" or skirt called a ***shendyt***. The shendyt typically came to just above the knee; most were white. Women wore a straight sheath dress called a ***kalasiris***, sometimes with a shawl over the shoulders. Both men and women wore clothing made from lightweight, sheer linen.

Women usually wore their hair long, frequently in micro braids. The favorite length seemed to be several inches past the shoulders, but sometimes waist length. Men either wore their hair short or shaven. They rarely wore beards. If they did, it was a goatee. Boys had shaved heads except for one lock on the side. The West Asian men in Egypt typically wore a full beard and a "mushroom-shaped," chin-length hairstyle with a headband.

We usually think of Egyptians with black hair, but the examination of mummies shows some Egyptians (even before the Greeks took over) had naturally red or light-brown hair. They also liked to dye their hair red with henna. Most Egyptians had wavy or curly hair, although a small number had straight hair. Dramatic eye makeup was essential to both men and women. They wore eyeliner of kohl, a crystalized lead sulfide. Their green eye shadow was made of malachite, a copper carbonate.

Women lute players wearing head cones, braids, and collar necklaces[30]

Egyptians of all classes loved wearing jewelry. Most women wore elaborate headbands. Some women wore head cones filled with scented wax. Their body heat melted the wax slightly, releasing the scent. Women liked to wear bracelets, armbands, and huge earrings. Both men and women wore large collar necklaces. If a person was wealthy, their collar necklace was turquoise or gold. Ordinary people wore collar necklaces made with pottery beads.

What Was Their Social Structure Like?

Ancient Egyptian society was, ironically, like a pyramid. At the bottom were the farmers and enslaved people, who made up most of the population. Almost all farmers were serfs who didn't own the land they farmed. Wealthy landowners bought and sold land, but the serfs stayed with the land regardless of who owned it. The next layer up were merchants and artisans. The artisans were artists, stone carvers, perfume makers, weavers, jewelry makers, and carpenters.

A sculpture of a fifth-dynasty scribe at Giza[21]

The third highest level was military men (except for officers) and scribes. Until the New Kingdom, the king would call up the farmers and other men to fight as needed. Egypt formed a full-time army after the embarrassment of being defeated by the foreign Hyksos.

A scribe had to learn about 700 signs to write basic hieroglyphics. It took twelve years of schooling. They were in demand by royalty, merchants, and anyone else needing something written down. Most Egyptians did not know how to read and write.

The fourth layer was priests and nobles who owned large pieces of property. The Egyptians had thousands of gods and goddesses, so there were plenty of openings for priests and priestesses. Before a priest could enter the temple, he had to bathe in holy water and shave off his body hair. An essential priestly duty was embalming dead bodies before burial.

The fifth layer up was government officials and top military officers, often part of the king's family. The top official was the vizier or advisor to the king. He organized the other officials and served as the supreme court judge. Other important officials were the commander of the military and the chief treasurer. At the top of the pyramid was the king, or pharaoh. Unlike in Syria, where a king was considered the shepherd or father of his people, the Egyptians thought their king was like a god.

Since they were semi-divine, pharaohs were intermediaries between the people and the gods. The sacred duties of a pharaoh included ensuring rain and good harvests, defending the country from invaders, and acting as an impartial judge. The Egyptians obeyed their king without asking questions. In their minds, disobeying their king would bring disorder and poverty to Egypt.

What about women? What was their role in society? First and foremost, they were wives and mothers. Ordinary people usually married for love, although the pharaohs had to make politically strategic marriages. The Egyptians believed their spouse would be their husband or wife in the afterlife. Thus, they worked to make the relationship thrive. They didn't want to spend eternity in an unhappy marriage!

An Egyptian couple harvesting papyrus [29]

As wives and mothers, ordinary Egyptian women tended the children, kept the house clean, and prepared meals. They wove linen from flax. Farmers' wives helped their husbands in the fields. More well-to-do women supervised the household servants and maybe ran a business like perfume making. Egyptian women also served as priestesses to female deities. Compared to their West Asian neighbors, they had more rights. They could own and sell property, be witnesses in court, and associate with men they weren't related to. Egyptian women had the right to divorce their husbands and get a third of their property.

What Religious Beliefs Did the Ancient Egyptians Follow?

Most of the ancient Egyptians were *polytheistic* (worshiping multiple gods). Some were the state gods, revered by the king and his priests at the national temples. The ordinary people had local deities that they worshiped. Egyptians also believed in supernatural creatures like the griffin and the sphinx. The griffin had a lion's body and an eagle's head and wings; it was a protector. The sphinx had a human head and a lion's body, representing the sun god.

Among the most important Egyptian gods were Amun, Mut, and Khonsu. The Egyptians believed that Amun was the creator of the universe and merged him with Ra, the sun god. Amun's wife was Mut, the mother goddess. Her paintings and statues often showed her wearing a bright red dress with vulture wings and holding an **ankh**, a cross with a circle at the top that symbolized life. Khonsu, the god of the moon, was her son. He was the god of healing and fertility and the destroyer of demons.

The Egyptian people's beliefs about their gods controlled how they lived and worked, their relationships with others, and their concept of life after death.

Everyone was supposed to follow *ma 'at*, or living in harmony. The Egyptians believed their actions

The goddess Mut[28]

impacted others and determined their fate in the afterlife. They had to live in balance and cooperation with each other so the gods could maintain order in the cosmos. The Egyptians considered most of their gods to be kind friends.

Heka (magic) was real to the Egyptians. In their belief system, everything that happened, good or bad, had a supernatural cause. Heka was a personification of Amun-Ra. He controlled medicine and magic and could blind crocodiles. Heka was a cosmic force that could be good or evil; he could protect but also destroy. Egyptians believed they could manipulate Heka through their words, actions, and particular objects. They used magic for protection.

How Did the Nile River Impact Egyptian Society and Culture?

The Nile was infinitely more than just a river for the Egyptian people. If it weren't for the Nile, Egypt would be a dry and dusty desert. Actually, parts of it are. Cairo only gets one-half inch of rain a year! The only reason Cairo isn't a desert is because it's right on the Nile, where it flows into the Nile Delta. Most of ancient Egypt's major cities were on the Nile or its delta region.

Vast swathes of Egypt were rich farmland, thanks to the Nile. It poured life into the desert. The river flooded every year, covering the surrounding area with rich black silt. Egypt could grow enough grain to feed its people, with plenty left over to sell to other lands. For the Egyptians, life and wealth flowed from the Nile; it provided for virtually every aspect of life. It was the primary means of travel through Egypt. Tomb art from the Old Kingdom shows boats carrying cattle, wood, and vegetables down the Nile. The Egyptians buried their kings with ships near their tombs.

A boat model from Egypt's Twelfth Dynasty [24]

The Nile was home to many animals. Fish provided an essential source of protein for Egyptians. Hippos and crocodiles thrived in the Nile River. Elephants lived along the Nile until climate change increased desertification in the Early Dynastic Period. Gazelles, cheetahs, and the Egyptian wolf roamed the mountains and plains on the edge of the Nile's floodplains. Barbary lions were common in the Nile Valley until they were overhunted in the New Kingdom. A small remnant survived into modern times, but the Barbary lion is now extinct.

The Egyptians based their calendar on the Nile's annual cycle. It had three seasons. The season from July to November when the river overflowed its banks was Akhet. Peret was the season for farming, which ran from November to March. The harvest season was Shemu. The Egyptians methodically tracked and recorded the annual floods each year.

The ancient Egyptian fields were "basins" surrounded by earthen banks. Channels ran from the Nile to the fields. When the river flooded, the fields filled with water. The basins held the water for a month until the soil was thoroughly saturated and ready for planting. The fields were so soggy the farmers didn't need to water the crops at all at first. When the fields finally dried out, the Egyptians had an ingenuous system of dikes and irrigation canals to channel the river water to the fields.

Is the Nile really the world's longest river? The Amazon River is a strong contender. Current measurements say the Nile is 4,132 miles and the Amazon is 3,977. However, some scientists say the source of the Amazon is in northern Peru, not southern Peru. An international team of explorers is planning expeditions to find out. They hope they can settle the debate soon.

How Did Art Reflect Their Culture?

Did you know that most of the ancient Egyptian art we've discovered was never meant to be seen? These paintings, wall carvings, and statues were inside tombs. What was the point of spending all that time creating exquisite art and then hiding it away? The art was there for the dead people or the gods they wanted to please. Many carvings and paintings had symbols like scorpions, snakes, or weapons. These were to protect from evil in the afterlife.

The Egyptians believed that art was a way to communicate with the gods. Some of the tomb art depicted the pharaoh or other high-ranking person going about his or her life. It showed the person offering sacrifices, winning great battles, or relaxing with family. The ancient Egyptians hoped the tomb art would come to life and the dead person would do these things in the afterlife.

Almost all Egyptian paintings and statues had "captions" or inscriptions naming the people depicted and often what was happening. Statues had inscriptions on the back or at the base. Paintings and reliefs carved into rock usually had writing underneath explaining the scene. They were written in hieroglyphics, an art form in itself. This custom has been helpful to archaeologists as it gives them names and dates to piece together Egypt's history and influential people.

Nefu, a Fifth Dynasty official in the Old Kingdom, and his wife[25]

One aspect of ancient Egyptian art was that proportions reflected status. Statues of important men and their wives often depict the husband towering over the woman. Was he an exceptionally tall man, or was his wife very short? More likely, the artist used proportion to demonstrate the man's importance. The man is also usually painted in brilliant colors, while the woman is pale. These statues are endearing, as the couples show physical affection. In the sculptures of royal children with their parents, they look like little dolls compared to the adults' size. Paintings of the pharaohs with servants or military men often show the king twice the size of everyone else.

What Was a Scarab?

As we mentioned earlier, in the Predynastic era, Egyptians adopted the cylinder seal from the Sumerians of southern Iraq. In the Middle Kingdom, the Egyptians switched to one-inch oval "scarabs" to identify themselves in letters or business transactions. This type of seal was modeled after the scarab beetle.

The beetle side of a scarab seal on a ring [26]

The scarab beetle is also known as a "dung" beetle. It eats poop! If it finds some, it shapes it into balls and rolls them to its nest. Why would the Egyptians want to make seals in the shape of this beetle? To the Egyptians, the dung ball symbolized the world. When the beetle rolled his ball of poop along, he kept the world spinning on its axis. The ancient Egyptians also thought the sun entered the underworld each night when it set and resurrected each morning as a scarab beetle. The Egyptians considered this humble beetle highly significant in the cycle of life.

The top of the scarab seal was rounded and looked like the beetle. The bottom was flat, with hieroglyphics carved into it to identify the owner. Like the cylinder seals, the owner pressed his or her scarab into a little ball of clay. It hardened to form its owner's "signature." The Egyptians liked to wear the seal on a ring so it would always be handy when they needed to use it. Thousands of these Egyptian beetle seals or their impressions have been found in Egypt, Israel, Palestine, and Syria. They open a window to how engaged specific pharaohs were in trade or colonies in other countries. They're also fascinating examples of art on a tiny scale.

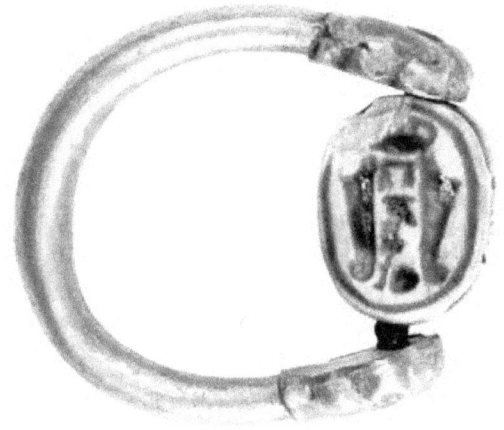

The back side of the scarab seal is pressed in clay. [27]

Roundup Activity: Fill in the Blank

Read the summary paragraph below. Fill in the blanks with the correct keyword. Check your answers in the back of the book.

The ancient Egyptians' favorite drink was _____, which they liked to drink through a straw. Because of the heat, they liked wearing lightweight clothing made from _____, which the ladies wove from flax. A scribe had to attend school for ____ years to learn all the hieroglyphic symbols. The Egyptians believed _____ was the creator of the universe. Egyptian artists used _____ to indicate the most important person in the painting or sculpture. The Egyptians thought the scarab beetle's dung ball represented the _____.

Chapter 4: Ancient Egyptian Architecture

When most people think of ancient Egyptian architecture, they picture the pyramids. Yet, the pyramids were mainly associated with the Old Kingdom. Ancient Egypt's palaces, temples, and other structures were also stunning. They showcased the imagination and incredible skill of Egypt's architects. Egypt's architecture displayed a pleasing balance of forms, reflecting the Egyptian's connection to their gods and their land.

King Khufu's solar ship [28]

The pyramids didn't stand out in the desert by themselves. A temple, a solar boat pit, and a palace often surrounded them. What is a solar boat? The Egyptians believed their king needed transportation in the afterlife. And when they thought of transportation, they thought of boats. After all, the Nile River was the primary means of getting from Upper to Lower Egypt. Several pyramids had a cedar-wood ship buried in a pit nearby. The ships were about 140 feet long with a cabin and oars. Some scholars think the king was transported to his tomb in the boat. However, the inscriptions at King Khufu's pyramid said that the solar ship carried his soul to the heavens.

How Were the Pyramids Built?

Many of Egypt's pyramids have lasted for 4,500 years! How did the Egyptians build them so well that they lasted so long? How did they build them without cranes and pullies and even the wheel? As we said, the Egyptians didn't have the wheel until the Fifth Dynasty, and the largest pyramid was erected in the Fourth Dynasty.

Did you know that the Great Pyramid had 2.3 *million* stone blocks? Each block weighed about 2.5 tons! To put that in perspective, that's about the weight of ten refrigerators. How did the workers get those blocks that high up in the air? Remember—the Great Pyramid was about 481 feet high. That's as high as a skyscraper with forty-eight stories. No wonder the Greek historian Herodotus put it on his list of the Seven Wonders of the Ancient World.

How could the workers complete such a massive feat in the lifetime of one king? It took a workforce of thousands of men. In 1992, NOVA produced a documentary called *This Old Pyramid*, in which they tried to replicate the effort of building even a small pyramid. They cheated a little. Those enormous blocks came in on flatbed trucks. However, the researchers were amazed that twelve men working barefoot in the eastern desert quarried 186 stones in 21 days. They didn't quite do everything the ancient way. They used an iron cable and winch to pull the stone out of the quarry. Still, the cutting and everything else was by hand.

Egyptologists Mark Lehner and Zahi Hawass did the math. Building the Great Pyramid in twenty years required 340 stones a day. How many men would it take to quarry those? Since the modern-day workers used iron tools and a winch, Hawass did his calculations based on thirty-two men instead of twelve. It took modern workers 21 days to deliver 186 stones, but the Great Pyramid needed 340 *daily*. They figured out that around 1,200 men could quarry 340 stones a day. The quarries for the core stones of the Giza pyramids were right there at Giza, so long-distance transportation wasn't an issue.

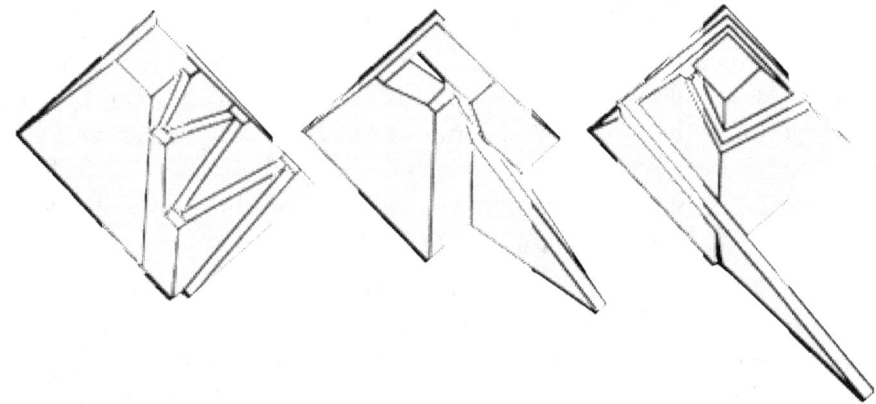

Three possible ramps were used to build the pyramids. The middle ramp is probably too steep. The zig-zag ramp on the left and the circular ramp on the right are more likely.²⁹

In their replication efforts, the *This Old Pyramid* team found twelve men could easily drag one colossal block on a giant sled over a slick surface. (Remember, they would wet down the sand to make it slippery.) The team estimated that it would take 1,200 men to cut stones in the quarry and around 2,000 men to drag them from the quarry to the pyramid. Once the stones arrived at the pyramid, a highly trained team cut them with great precision. They fit together so tightly a knife blade couldn't slide between two stones.

The NOVA experiment demonstrated what had to happen to carve a 2.5-ton block. Four to six men labored on one stone at a time. Two men worked with levers and a hard cobble under a block to pivot it around. Two to four people did the cutting. Researchers estimated it took about 5,000 men to do this job. They believe one team worked from each corner of the pyramid, and the middle of each face of the pyramid had another team.

The workers used the inclined plane (a sloping surface) to move the blocks up the pyramid on ramps. In addition to the granite blocks used in the pyramid's core, the outside had a layer of fine white limestone, polished so that it glistened in the sun. This limestone was quarried in Tura and shipped to Giza, about ten miles by way of the Nile.

Who Built the Pyramids?

Despite what you might have seen in old movies, it wasn't the Jews or any other foreign enslaved people who built the pyramids. The pyramids were built during the Old Kingdom. The Jews did not exist at that time since Abraham hadn't been born yet.

So, who were the thousands of men who built each of the massive pyramids? The Old Kingdom pyramids, including the Great Pyramid, were built by native Egyptians. The whole idea of a pyramid was to provide for the future afterlife of their king, who they believed became a god. From the Egyptians' perspective, their toil on the pyramids blessed Egypt and blessed their own future in the afterlife.

The most likely scenario was that a smaller crew of men worked year-round. From July to November, when the Nile overflowed its banks, the farmers didn't have much to do. Most were probably sent to work on the pyramids during those months. They worked in teams, and archaeologists have found where the teams signed their "tribal" names on the inner stones of the pyramids. One team called themselves the "Drunkards of Menkaure." They undoubtedly enjoyed a few rounds of beer when they finished the day's work! Other teams were named "Friends of Khufu" and "The Powerful Ones."

Pyramids at Giza[80]

Men working this hard needed a good protein source. Animal bones at the site and surviving records indicate cattle were brought in from the

Nile Delta region. Of course, sustaining this immense army of workers required another team of bakers and cooks to feed them. Archaeologists have unearthed bakeries that fed the workers at Giza.

They also found a cemetery where 600 people were buried. Archaeologists and doctors analyzed the skeletons of the workers in that cemetery, and they were Egyptians. Most of them died in their early thirties, and some died from accidents. Twelve of the workers had received treatment for earlier injuries to their hands or legs, where a stone had fallen on them. Amazingly, they lived for years after the treatment and must have continued working since they were buried right there.

What Was the Significance of the Pyramids?

The pyramids represented several aspects of ancient Egyptian culture. Egyptians believed in *ba*, which was a part of the soul. Only the king had a ba in the Old Kingdom, but later, everyone did. Ba appeared as a bird with a human head, representing the soul's flight after death. He could fly from Earth to the heavens, but he needed a landmark when he flew back to Earth. The pyramid guided him back to his mortal body.

Ba[81]

The Egyptians believed that the smooth sides and pointed peak of a pyramid guided the king's soul (ba) to the sun god Ra in the sky. The triangular sides represented the sun's rays. The Egyptians believed that ba left the body after death, but another aspect of the king's soul, *ka*, stayed in his mummified body. Thus, the priests would store goods he would need and bring more food from time to time. The pyramid was like a palace for the king's earth-bound ka.

The shape of the pyramids not only lifted one's eyes to the heavens but also had a practical side. The Egyptians intended their pyramids to endure forever. The smooth, polished, slanted sides allowed the little bit of rain that fell to run off quickly without eroding the structure. The pyramid shape also held up well to high winds.

Whenever merchant ships or ambassadors from other lands sailed down the Nile, they passed the majestic pyramids. The pyramids were a status symbol, showcasing Egypt's power and wealth. They spoke to the incredible workforce Egypt commanded and how the kings could unify tens of thousands of their citizens toward the single goal.

The Iconic Great Pyramid of Giza

The Pyramids of Giza are a cluster of pyramids built by several kings between 2600 and 2181 BCE. The Great Pyramid was built first. It was the largest of the group and the highest pyramid ever built in the world. King Khufu started its construction around 2550 BCE. When it was built, polished white limestone blocks encased all four sides of the pyramid. After earthquakes in 1356 CE, the Mamluk Sultanate stripped some of these casing stones off the pyramid and used them to repair buildings in Cairo. In the nineteenth century, the Ottoman governor Muhammad Ali Pasha took more outer stones to build Cairo's Alabaster Mosque. Almost all the casing stones are gone today. All that is left is the core structure, which is about 454 feet high, around 27 feet shorter than the original pyramid.

What's inside the Great Pyramid? It has three primary chambers. One is King Khufu's burial tomb. Another is the "Queen's Chamber," and the third is the Subterranean Chamber. The pyramid has numerous corridors snaking through its core and shafts going underground. Usually, the Egyptians painted the inner walls of their pyramids, but the Great Pyramid's inside is unpainted. Perhaps Khufu died before the artists had time to paint pictures on the walls. The only thing left on the inside walls is the graffiti of the work teams.

The workers cut the Subterranean Chamber into the bedrock about eighty-nine feet under the pyramid. This room was unfinished, again hinting that the pyramid was incomplete when Khufu died. What was the Subterranean Chamber used for? Scholars are uncertain. Some think it was meant to be Khufu's tomb, but plans changed when he died earlier than expected. Other scholars believe he may have changed his mind and wanted to be buried higher in the pyramid. The so-called Queen's Chamber may have also been intended for Khufu. At any rate, it appears that no one was buried there.

Granite slabs line the walls of the King's Chamber, Khufu's burial place. Over the millennia, robbers broke into the pyramid multiple times. The only thing left in Khufu's tomb is his granite sarcophagus, a stone coffin. The only reason the robbers left the sarcophagus was that it was too big to fit around the corner of the tight passage coming into the chamber. The ancient workers must have lowered Khufu's coffin into his chamber from above, then finished the roof of the chamber to seal it in.

Giza's Great Sphinx

Khufu's son, Khafre, built the second-largest pyramid at Giza. It seems higher than the Great Pyramid, but that's because it's on slightly higher ground with steeper sides. It stands 448 feet high compared to Khufu's (now) 454-foot pyramid. Khafre's pyramid still has some of its limestone casing. Grave robbers also raided Khafre's tomb and took his mummy and everything except his red granite sarcophagus.

When the Italian adventurer Giovanni Belzoni found the burial chamber in 1818 CE, he discovered writings in Arabic. They said that the tomb was opened during the reign of King Ali Muhammad, around 1200 CE. Weirdly, he found cattle bones in the burial chamber. Who put those there, when, and why? That mystery is unanswered.

The Great Sphinx of Giza[38]

Khafre's pyramid is famous for the hulking statue of a sphinx next to it, which has Khafre's head and the body of a lion. Over the millennia, the blowing desert sands covered the Great Sphinx until only its head stuck out. When archaeologists dug it out in the 1800s, they discovered that workers had never completed the lower part of the statue. It is 240 feet long and 66 feet high, as tall as a six-story building. Its artists carved the entire sculpture from one piece of limestone. The pigment on the ancient statue shows it was brightly painted in blue, yellow, and red when first erected. As artisans carved the sphinx statue, they used the blocks they chiseled off to build a temple in front of it. The Great Sphinx probably represented King Khafre offering sacrifices to his father, Khufu.

Why Did the Egyptians Stop Building Pyramids?

Pyramids built later in the Old Kingdom were smaller and of poorer quality. Egypt started running out of the wealth and manpower needed to create these extraordinary monuments. An intriguing detail of the later pyramids, beginning with that of King Unas, who died around 2345 BCE, was the inscriptions inside the pyramids. The walls were covered with the oldest known Egyptian religious texts. The purpose of these texts was to guide the king out of his tomb and into his new life with the gods.

The last sizeable pyramid was for Pepy II, who died around 2184 BCE. His pyramid was only 172 feet high. Shortly after his death, the Old Kingdom collapsed. Some Middle Kingdom kings and one New Kingdom pharaoh built pyramids, but they were much smaller.

The Hyksos Dynasty was infamous for blatant tomb robbing. They sold the stolen goods to the kings of Lebanon, who buried the stolen purloined treasures in their own graves.

What Other Astounding Architecture Did Ancient Egyptians Build?

In the Middle and New Kingdoms, the Egyptians focused on building temples rather than pyramids. Many of these temples have survived. They have incredible detail and beauty. One amazing example is the temple complex of Amun-Re and the Hypostyle Hall at Karnak near Thebes. The Egyptians built this temple in the Middle Kingdom and added to it in the New Kingdom. It was the worship center for Amun, his wife Mut, and the falcon-headed god of the military, Montu.

Painted columns at Luxor Temple[88]

The Karnak Temple Complex is one of the world's largest, with over twenty temples in its central worship area. A forest of 134 massive columns supported the roof of the Hypostyle Hall, a breathtaking open-air worship area. The roof in the hall's center was higher, with 69-foot columns. Over 600 sphinxes lined the 1.7-mile Avenue of the Sphinxes connecting the Karnak Temple with the Luxor Temple. The Luxor Temple featured a bright blue ceiling and brilliant red, gold, and sky blue columns.

Another spectacular architectural feature of ancient Egyptian temples was obelisks. These were towering rectangular stone pillars with a pointed top like a pyramid. Incredibly, they were carved from one huge stone. They served as the prototype for the Washington Monument in Washington, D.C. This striking architecture dates to the Predynastic Era in Egypt. The Egyptians built obelisks to honor an important king, a god, or a special event. The Egyptians often built a pair of obelisks together at the entrance to temples.

The Temple of Luxor entrance once had a second obelisk on the right.[54]

Roundup Activity: Build Your Own Pyramid!

Pretend you're an ancient Egyptian queen or king. Design and draw your pyramid. You can draw a sphinx by the pyramid with your face and a lion's body. If you want to get super creative, you can design the tunnels and chambers inside the pyramid. You might want to include landscape features nearby, like palm trees or the Nile River.

Chapter 5: The Afterlife: Exploring Life after Death in Ancient Egypt

As we explore the complex world of ancient Egyptian religion, we will first dive into the roles of gods and goddesses. What did the Egyptians believe about their deities? Who were Anubis, Ra, and Osiris, and how were they involved in the afterlife? What did the Egyptians think happened after they died? How did they prepare for the next life? What were mummies and the Book of the Dead all about? Let's unwrap the answers to these questions and more.

What Roles Did the Gods and Goddesses Play?

The ancient Egyptians believed in thousands of gods but had about thirty primary deities. They each had a specific role and special powers. For instance, the Egyptians believed some deities had the power to create. Others controlled the weather and the annual flooding of the Nile, which was crucial for growing enough food. Some gods protected people, animals, and even plants. Other gods cared for people after they died. Most towns and cities had a patron god who looked after the people there.

The Egyptians considered most of their gods friendly and helpful. However, they had several super scary gods. One of Egypt's cat goddesses was named Mafdet. She protected people from poisonous snakes but was also the goddess of executions. She was usually pictured as a woman with a cat head and snakes flowing down her back instead of hair. Ahti was a creepy goddess with a hippopotamus body and a wasp head. She was spiteful, harmful to children, and didn't seem to offer any benefit to humans. Another goddess with a hippo body was Taweret, the bizarre goddess of fertility, motherhood, and nursing infants. She had crocodile jaws, a hippopotamus body, a woman's breasts, and lion legs and claws.

Taweret, goddess of motherhood[85]

Amun was the Egyptian god of creation. He and eight of his children, grandchildren, and great-grandchildren formed the Ennead, the nine most powerful deities in Heliopolis, a key religious center near today's Cairo. Other places in Egypt had different groupings of the deities they considered the most important. The chief gods tended to change in importance over the thousands of years of ancient Egypt's history.

A favorite Egyptian goddess was Isis, the wife of Osiris and mother of Horus. She was first worshiped in the Nile Delta region, but eventually, almost everyone in Egypt honored her. The Egyptians believed that, in a sense, Isis was the mother of all the pharaohs because they thought their kings were earthly representations of Horus. One of her titles was Weret-Kekau, or "Great Magic." She was among the deities who made the Nile flood each year.

Isis with the New Kingdom Pharaoh Haremhab[86]

What Was the King's Role in Religion?

The Egyptians thought their king had godlike status, so he was the middleman between heaven and earth. Egypt had many priests, but the king was the head of both religion and the government. Thus, he worked to ensure harmony in his land and led religious ceremonies. The Egyptians knew their king was mortal and that he would die one day. However, as we said, they considered him the living representative of the god Horus. After he died, he became Osiris, the god of the underworld.

Parts of the Human Soul

As we mentioned in chapter four, the ancient Egyptians thought their souls had multiple parts. Ba was the personality or the person's true essence. This part of the soul left the body after death, and if all went well, the person continued existing in ba form in the underworld. A ren was a person's secret name, which needed to be remembered so the soul could continue to exist after death. Ka was another part of the soul that stayed on earth after the person died. As you may remember from our discussion of the pyramids, the ancient Egyptians left food and other things to keep this part of the soul fed and happy. The ib was the person's heart or morality. Shut was the person's shadow, a reflection of his or her personhood. Egyptian art sometimes showed the soul leaving the tomb in the form of a shadow.

What Offering Rites Did the Egyptians Follow?

The Egyptians believed they needed to honor their gods and goddesses, even the ones with bad tempers who looked like extraterrestrials. If the Egyptians kept the deities happy, life was smooth. If they got on their bad side, violence and destruction would hunt them down. Thus, priests and priestesses of every temple made offerings to the gods daily. These sacrifices included drink, food, ointment, and clothing for temple idols. They did not think the idols themselves were gods but visible representations of divine forces.

Before the priests approached the temple, they burned incense. Then, they broke a seal and untied the cords holding the door of the temple or shrine shut. The priests approached the god's image, kissed the ground before its feet, and raised their arms while singing hymns. They went down on their belly in front of the god's image, stretching their arms out on the ground. Finally, they anointed the idol with scented oil and burned incense before it.

Who Were Anubis, Ra, and Osiris?

Anubis, Ra, and Osiris were the Egyptian gods of the dead. The black jackal god Anubis was the god of mummification and funeral rites. He stood at the gates of the underworld with his scales. As dead souls approached, Anubis weighed their hearts with an ostrich feather on the other side of the scale. Which weighed more? A person who had lived a life of harmony and peace had a heart as light as a feather. This person could enter **Duat**, the underworld, with Anubis guiding their souls. However, Ammit, the "Devourer of the Dead," ate the people with hearts weighed down by disorder and constant arguments. She had a crocodile head, and her body was half lioness and half hippo.

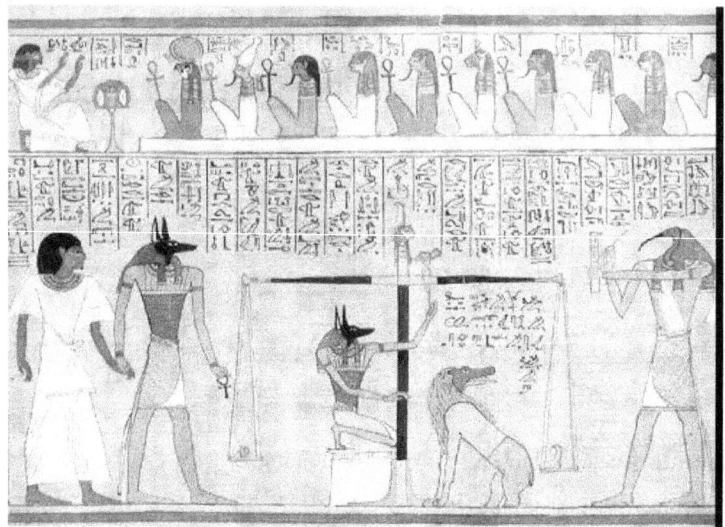

Anubis weighs a heart as Ammit waits to eat those who don't measure up.⁸⁷

The sun god Ra was one of ancient Egypt's most important deities. The Egyptians combined him with Amun, the creator. He traveled across the sky by day but passed through Duat at night. Every night in the underworld, he had to fight Apep, the serpent god of chaos. Apep wanted to keep Ra from rising again because the world would die without the sun. When Amun-Ra defeated Apep each night, he restored order and brought life and warmth back to the world as he sailed through the sky.

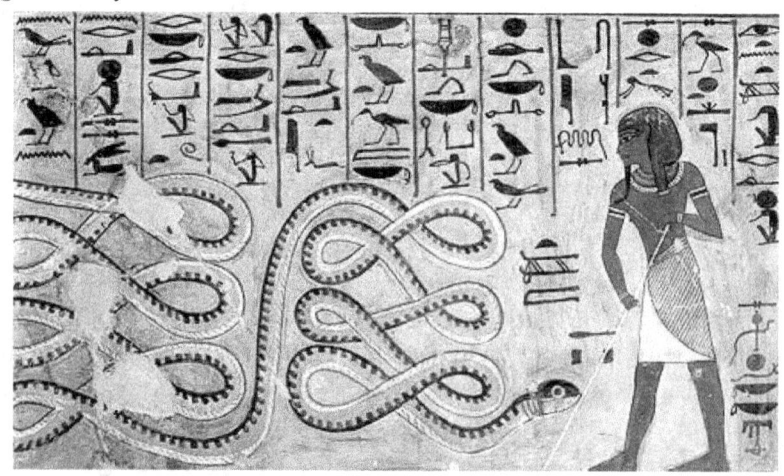

Amun-Ra fights the serpent Apep. ⁸⁸

Osiris was the god of fertility and agriculture. He got into an argument with his brother Set (Seth), who killed him and chopped him into pieces. Osiris was married to his sister, Isis. She went looking for her brother-husband and found the pieces of his body. She put them back together and wrapped him up in strips of cloth, forming the first mummy. Isis used her superpowers to bring Osiris back to life long enough to get pregnant with their son Horus. However, she couldn't keep him in the land of the living, so Osiris became the god of the underworld. He is portrayed with the green skin of a decomposing person.

How Did the Egyptians Prepare for the Afterlife?

Ancient Egyptians knew they wouldn't automatically enter Duat, the underworld. After they died, the Egyptians believed they had to fend off horrifying demons on their journey to the place of judgment. When they arrived, they first had to list all the sins they had *not* committed in their lifetime. If they passed that test, then Anubis weighed their hearts. The ones whose hearts were lighter than a feather began their journey to **Aaru**.

To get to Aaru, they had to pass through many gates guarded by frightening gods and demons. After they passed through the gates, they reached Aaru by boat. Aaru meant the "Field of Reeds," a lush place like the Nile Delta where they could grow plenty of food. Aaru had thousands of islands of reeds surrounded by water, so it was a wonderful place for hunting and fishing.

The ancient Egyptians knew they had to prepare in their lifetime for their eventual journey into the underworld. They needed certain things to protect and guide them to the place of judgment and through the gates to Aaru. Before they died, they collected magic amulets and writings from the Book of the Dead. **Amulets** were jewelry items they believed had special powers to protect and bring good luck. Most people had a **heart scarab** carved before they died, crafted with the same shape as the scarab seals. After death, it was placed on their chest before they were mummified. The scarab beetle represented the cycle of life and rebirth.

If they were lucky enough to make it to Aaru, the Egyptians thought they would have to work in the fields to grow food. Many Egyptians would bury **shabtis**, or little dolls, with them. These came to life when an incantation was spoken over them, and they did the work for the dead person in the afterlife. The rich buried hundreds of shabtis with them, ensuring they would never have to work.

What Was the Book of the Dead?

The Book of the Dead was a collection of writings about magic spells and other essential information a dead person would need on their way to Duat. The Egyptians thought they had a difficult journey to the afterworld when their souls left their bodies, and the Book of the Dead was their guidebook. They needed to know which incantations to chant to fight the demons. They also required directions for how to pass through the underworld and make sure they made it to Aaru.

These spells were written on papyrus scrolls, a paper-like material made from the reed-like papyrus plant that grew in water. Egyptians also used the Book of the Dead to guide their funeral practices in the New Kingdom. The Egyptian title meant "Coming Forth into the Day," reflecting the Egyptian belief that death was not the end but a transition to a new life.

Nauny (second on the left) stands in judgment before Osiris on his throne.³⁹

Archaeologists found one of the papyrus scrolls in the Book of the Dead buried with Nauny, the chantress of Amun-Ra. A chantress was a priestess who sang or chanted songs and spells to the gods. Every day, she awakened the god in its temple by singing to it, then put it to sleep in the evening the same way. A chantress also served at funerals. She would sing the spells over the dead person to guide him or her to Duat. A chantress was usually a princess or from an upper-class family. Nauny was the king's daughter, and she died in her seventies.

The Book of the Dead scroll buried with Nauny was inside a wooden idol of Osiris. When unrolled, it was over seventeen feet long. The scroll was full of pictures and numerous magic spells for each part of the journey to Duat. In one image, Nauny stands before Anubis as he weighs her heart. Isis stands behind Nauny, and Osiris sits on a throne overseeing the judgment, wrapped up like a mummy. In front of him is a joint of beef that has been sacrificed as part of Nauny's funeral. A baboon sits on top of the scales, writing down the results. He is Thoth, the god of writing and wisdom. Did Nauny pass the test? Yes! Anubis reports to Osiris that her heart is a good witness.

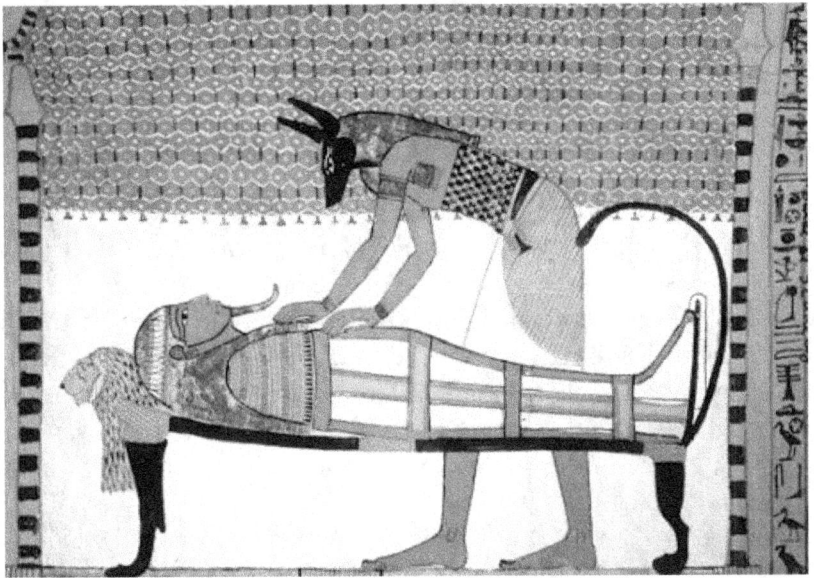

A priest representing Anubis prepares a mummy.[40]

Why and How Did They Mummify the Dead?

Because the ancient Egyptians believed the ka aspect of the soul continued to live in or near the person's body after they died, they embalmed the body so it would not decay. The god Anubis who weighed people's hearts was also the god of mummification. Special priests representing Anubis performed the embalming process. The first step in mummification was removing the person's body organs. The heart stayed in the body, but the brain was pulled out through the nose with hooks. The lungs, liver, stomach, and intestines were also removed.

These organs went into jars full of natron salt, which dried them out. Sometimes, the priests buried these jars with the mummies. Other times, they reinserted the dried organs into the body and sewed it up. They also covered the body in natron salt for seventy days to dry it. Once the body and organs dried out, the priests washed the body and rubbed oil over the skin. Next, they rubbed black resin over the whole body. After this, they wrapped the entire body in strips of linen, turning it into a mummy.

The priests decorated the mummy with jewelry and placed particular charms on the body to protect it. They usually put a mask over the head of royalty. When the mummy was ready to be buried, they placed it in a wooden coffin. If the dead person was royalty, a high official, or a priest, they set their coffin inside a massive stone sarcophagus. The coffin or sarcophagus then went into a tomb with things the person needed in the afterlife, like furniture, mirrors, clothing, food, drink, and games.

What Kind of Funerary Rites Did the Egyptians Follow for the Dead?

The ancient Egyptians thought tombs were portals through which the dead could travel between the land of the living and the underworld. Many pharaohs and distinguished Egyptians were buried on the Nile's west bank near Luxor in a place called the Valley of the Kings. A dramatic funerary rite that the Egyptians followed was sailing decorated funeral barges along this section of the Nile. They portrayed Ra's journey through the underworld at night and back into the sky during the day.

Burial of the New Kingdom scribe Hunefer. His wife and daughter mourn while a priest in an Anubis mask supports his mummified body. Other priests chant incantations.[41]

The priests held an important funerary rite after the dead person was mummified and just before he or she was buried. They gathered with the deceased person's family in front of the tomb for the "Opening of the Mouth" ceremony. In this ritual, a priest wore a jackal mask representing Anubis. He held the mummy in a standing position while the family mourned in front of the dead body. Meanwhile, other priests burned incense and offered the body food and clothing. Once this ceremony ended, the priests placed the mummy in the tomb's burial chamber.

Roundup Activity: Pop Quiz

Check your answers in the back of the book.
1. Who was the goddess of fertility and motherhood?
2. What did the ancient Egyptians believe happened to the ka part of the soul after death?
3. What was the role of the king in ancient Egyptian religion?
4. Why did the Egyptians consider Isis the "mother of the pharaohs"?
5. What god weighed the hearts of dead people?
6. Who was the god of the sun and one of the most important deities in ancient Egyptian religion?
7. How did Osiris become the god of the underworld?
8. Why did the ancient Egyptians bury shabti dolls with a dead person?
9. What was the purpose of the Book of the Dead?
10. What ceremony was held just before placing a mummy in its tomb?

Chapter 6: Hatshepsut: The Female Pharaoh

Of Egypt's handful of women kings, Hatshepsut stood out as one of the most powerful in ancient Egyptian history. Hatshepsut was among Egypt's greatest pharaohs, men or women. In her thirteen years as pharaoh, she restored wealth to Egypt and graced the land with breathtaking new monuments and artwork. Hatshepsut claimed to be a half-goddess, the daughter of Amun.

What Happened in the Early Years of the New Kingdom?

Who ruled Egypt's New Kingdom before Hatshepsut? Ahmose I, who successfully chased the Hyksos from Egypt to Syria, began the New Kingdom (1550-1100 BCE) and the Eighteenth Dynasty (1550-1292 BCE). He re-unified Egypt and made Thebes the capital of Egypt again.

Ahmose also regained command over Nubia (northern Sudan) to the south. The ancient Egyptians had always wanted access to Nubia's fantastically rich gold mines. Egypt's gold stores became legendary in the New Kingdom. A Mitanni king commented, "Gold occurs in Egypt like sand on the roads." Ahmose built the last pyramid in Egypt for a native ruler.

Amenhotep I became the next pharaoh at around age fourteen in 1526 BCE. He wasn't supposed to be king, but his older brothers died young. His mother, Ahmose-Nefertari, ruled as regent until he came of age. Amenhotep's court astronomer, Amenemheb, invented the first water clock. It was a stone vessel with sloping sides and a small hole at the bottom through which water dripped. The inside of the bowl had twelve lines marking the hours as the water slowly receded. Time could be measured by the sun during the daylight hours, but the water clock was useful at night. The priests needed to perform the necessary sacrifices at the right time.

Amenhotep I[10]

During Amenhotep I's reign, Egyptian doctors wrote the Ebers Papyrus, possibly copied from earlier texts. What was in this ancient medical book? For one, it had magic spells to cast out demons, as the ancient Egyptians believed evil spirits caused migraines and other medical problems. They often called these demons crocodiles in their spells.

However, exorcism wasn't the only treatment plan. The Ebers Papyrus described how to use herbal medicine for many conditions. It taught that the body has twenty-two vessels carrying blood, mucus, tears, and semen. Doctors believed that a blockage of any of these vessels caused disease. The ancient Egyptians also understood that the heart provided the body's blood supply. The Ebers Papyrus instructed doctors to take the patient's pulse to check the condition of the heart.

Ancient Egyptian doctors could diagnose cancer and diabetes, yet how they did it is unclear. The Ebers Papyrus also discussed mental illnesses like depression and dementia. It included methods of contraception and how to diagnose a pregnancy and gave instructions for setting broken bones and treating burns.

None of Amenhotep's children survived infancy, so Thutmose I became the next pharaoh. Thutmose was most likely Amenhotep's brother-in-law. His primary wife ("the Great Royal Wife") was also named Ahmose, so she may have been the daughter of Amenhotep and Ahmose-Nefertari. Thutmose arranged Ahmose-Nefertari's burial, not her son Amenhotep. She probably died after Amenhotep, and Thutmose was possibly her son-in-law. Thutmose's mother was Senseneb, a non-royal.

Thutmose I and his mother, Senseneb[48]

Thutmose I launched military campaigns in West Asia, conquering Canaan, Lebanon, and the kingdom of Qatna in Syria. He built a victory monument at Carchemish, on the border of today's Turkey and Syria. He also expanded Egypt's borders south to the Fourth Cataract of the Nile, in today's Sudan. His military conquests opened up robust trade and brought staggering riches to Egypt.

Thutmose I and Ahmose were the parents of Hatshepsut. They also had two sons and another daughter. The sons died before Thutmose did. Thutmose had a minor wife named Mutnofret, the mother of Thutmose II. Before he died, Thutmose arranged the marriage of Hatshepsut to her half-brother, Thutmose II. Hatshepsut was only twelve at the time. As the daughter of the "Great Royal Wife," Hatshepsut brought a higher level of royalty and credibility to Thutmose II.

Thutmose II's generals dealt with uprisings in Nubia, Canaan, and Syria. He did not seem to ride out to war himself, perhaps because he was too young. Thutmose II and his half-sister Hatshepsut had a daughter named Neferure, probably their only child. With a woman in his harem named Isis, Thutmose II had a son, Thutmose III. Thutmose II died around age thirty when Thutmose III, his only heir, was two years old.

How Did Hatshepsut Rise to Power?

Thutmose II's early death left a power vacuum in Egypt. Officially, Thutmose III was the next pharaoh, but who would rule as his regent while he grew up? His mother, Isis, was just a concubine in the harem. She wasn't royal, so she wouldn't do. Hatshepsut became the regent for her husband's son.

At first, she was a conventional regent, taking care of matters of state in his name. For the first few years, Thutmose III was clearly the only pharaoh of Egypt. But things took a dramatic turn in Thutmose III's seventh year as pharaoh. The boy was only nine or ten, still too young to rule independently. Suddenly, Hatshepsut began calling herself by a pharaoh's titles. She took the full powers of a king as a co-ruler with her step-son. Why? Did unbridled ambition drive Hatshepsut, or was something else at play?

Hatshepsut

Some Egyptologists believe that someone threatened Thutmose's throne. Perhaps another branch of the family was making a move to snatch power. They might have argued that it would still be another decade before the boy was grown. Egypt needed an adult to deal with any crises. So, Hatshepsut may have stepped into the pharaoh's role to preserve the throne for her stepson. However, even when he came of age, she stayed on the throne. They co-ruled Egypt for fifteen years until Hatshepsut died.

Of course, Hatshepsut's power play shocked Egypt. She went to great lengths to defend her legitimacy to rule Egypt as a full pharaoh. She pointed out that she had more royal blood than anyone else in the family—and not just royal blood but divine blood as well! The custom in those days was for the pharaoh's wife or daughter to take the title "God's Wife of Amun." This title meant she was a priestess of the creator god. Hatshepsut assisted Amun's high priest by singing and dancing at rituals.

But then, Hatshepsut claimed that Amun was not just her spiritual husband but also her biological father. She said that before she was born, Amun took on an incarnation as Thutmose I. Amun found Hatshepsut's mother, Ahmose, asleep in her beautiful palace. The divine fragrance wafting off of Amun awakened Ahmose. When she saw the god, she thought he was her husband.

Ahmose's beauty aroused Amun, and he slept with her as the scent of perfume filled the palace. Afterward, he revealed his true identity.

As the daughter of Amun, the king of the gods, Hatshepsut elevated herself to half-divine status. No one else could compete or question her right to rule. Furthermore, Hatshepsut claimed that her father, the god Amun, had prophesied that she would rule Upper and Lower Egypt and all the foreign lands under Egypt's control.

To further cement her position as pharaoh, Hatshepsut went through a gender transition—at least her paintings and statues did. Since the Egyptians were adamant that their pharaoh should be a man, her images became more masculine. After she appointed herself co-pharaoh with Thutmose III, artwork showed her wearing men's clothing, with small breasts and a more muscular build. Sometimes, she had a beard or the shadow of a mustache over her lips.

Hatshepsut with a beard and male clothing[45]

Who Was Senenmut?

Hatshepsut knew that to keep power, she had to have supporters in key positions. Senenmut had been steward to Hatshepsut and her daughter, Neferure, and was a trusted friend. In the New Kingdom, a royal steward oversaw the pharaohs' land and was in charge of food for the palace. After becoming co-pharaoh with her stepson, Hatshepsut made Senenmut her chief minister and architect.

As chief architect, Senenmut was responsible for cutting and installing four pink granite obelisks in Hatshepsut's honor at the Temple of Karnak. They were the tallest in the world at that time, standing over ninety feet. Carving a single obelisk in one piece out of stone took seven months. One obelisk still stands today. Senenmut may also have been an astronomer. The oldest Egyptian star map is on the ceiling of his tomb.

Senenmut holding Princess Neferure on his lap[46]

What Did Hatshepsut Accomplish as Pharaoh?

Hatshepsut immediately set to work on building projects. She was so enthusiastic about building things that she accomplished more construction programs than any other pharaoh except Ramesses II. She sent military campaigns to Syria and Nubia, although her reign was mainly peaceful. Syria was Egypt's northern border through much of the New Kingdom, and the pharaohs often had to fight the Canaanites or Syrians to maintain that claim.

Hatshepsut falsely claimed that the Hyksos had destroyed Egyptian temples and burned down cities. She said she restored the damage. However, Ahmose had sent the Hyksos packing over seven decades earlier. None of the four kings before her mentioned devastation left by the Hyksos, nor does archaeology show this, except for a palace that burned in Avaris. And it was almost certainly a West Asian palace, not Egyptian.

Hatshepsut sent a sailing expedition of thousands of men down the Red Sea to Punt, also known as "God's Land." Where was Punt? Scholars have argued this question for centuries. It is well documented as an actual place, but apparently, the ancient inscribers assumed everyone knew where it was. Pictures of Punt painted by the Egyptians show houses built on stilts and surrounded by palm trees. The land had giraffes, leopards, baboons, and rhinos.

One clue is that the journey began by ship down the Red Sea. Another clue is what they got from Punt. The Egyptians traded for a treasure trove of gold, ebony, and myrrh. They also got wood from Punt—a rare resource in Egypt's desert lands—and electrum, a gold and silver alloy. A third clue is that they could also get there via the Nile (when they had friendly relations with Nubia), so Punt must have been somewhere in East Africa.

What Was Exceptional About Her Mortuary Temple at Deir el-Bahri?

Senenmut was the mastermind who designed Hatshepsut's mortuary temple on the Nile's west bank near Luxor. A mortuary temple was not a person's tomb. Instead, it was a place built near the tomb to worship the dead pharaoh and bring food and other offerings. Every day, priests performed rituals to honor the dead.

The mortuary temple designed by Senenmut was cut into the face of a cliff. The temple had reflecting pools, terraced gardens, and three layers of graceful colonnades. Sphinxes lined the walkways, and stone lions guarded the doorways. Everything was beautifully balanced and in harmony.

Hatshepsut's mortuary temple at the base of a cliff

Did Thutmose III Continue Ruling after Hatshepsut Died?

Hatshepsut died in her late forties, around 1460 BCE, when Thutmose III was twenty-one. Thutmose ruled Egypt by himself for three more decades. Three months after Hatshepsut died, he led his first known military campaign to Megiddo in northern Canaan. Thutmose scored a jaw-dropping victory against a coalition of Canaanite and Syrian kings. It was the beginning of a stellar military career. Egypt's warrior king won at least seventeen campaigns and captured 350 cities.

Thutmose had to choose one of three possible routes as he approached Megiddo. His war council warned him not to take the narrow middle path, as it was slower and dangerous. But he chose that route anyway, riding his chariot in front until the pass became so narrow that his chariot couldn't fit through. The Egyptians took their chariots apart and carried them as they marched in single file. By taking the narrow path, they caught the Canaanites by surprise.

Thutmose III[48]

However, the Hurrians of the Mitanni Kingdom in Syria and Turkey were growing strong and overconfident. They made the mistake of raiding Egypt's territory in Syria. Thutmose III launched another surprise attack. His men carried boats inland and crossed the northern Euphrates River into Mitanni land. The Hurrians weren't expecting him to show up so suddenly and had no time to organize a defense. Their princes huddled fearfully in caves as the Egyptians laid waste to their cities.

Thutmose III had at least seven wives. Three wives were probably Syrian princesses, and their names were Menwi, Merti, and Menhet.

They were buried together in a lavish tomb. They all seem to have died around the same time, perhaps of some epidemic. Another wife was Merytre-Hatshepsut, an Egyptian noblewoman. She and Thutmose had six children, including Amenhotep II, who became the next pharaoh.

What Happened to Hatshepsut's Monuments and Images after Her Death?

What was the dynamic between Hatshepsut and Thutmose III? It's hard to tell. He was a child or teenager for most of her reign, and he left no inscriptions that said anything negative about Hatshepsut. Nevertheless, about twenty years after her death, he went to great lengths to erase her memory. Workers cut her images off walls and plastered over her name in places it appeared. Thutmose ordered her statues to be torn down, defaced, and buried in a pit.

However, he did not harm things hidden away in her tomb. He only focused on official records and what could be seen in public. He was so thorough that Hatshepsut was the forgotten pharaoh for thousands of years. No one knew she existed until the 1800s CE when Egyptologist Jean-François Champollion decoded the texts in her tomb.

Did Thutmose III resent that Hatshepsut had usurped his throne? Maybe, but he became the full pharaoh at age twenty-one, anyway. He had a long and successful career. Why wait twenty years after her death to remove her memory? Perhaps he wanted to ensure stability and order in Egypt's royal line. After all, pharaohs were supposed to be men, and the king was the earthly representation of the god Horus. Eliminating Hatshepsut from the record left a tidy, unbroken line of male kings, from Thutmose I to Thutmose II to Thutmose III.

Roundup Activity: Crossword

Check your answers in the back of the book.

Who or where?

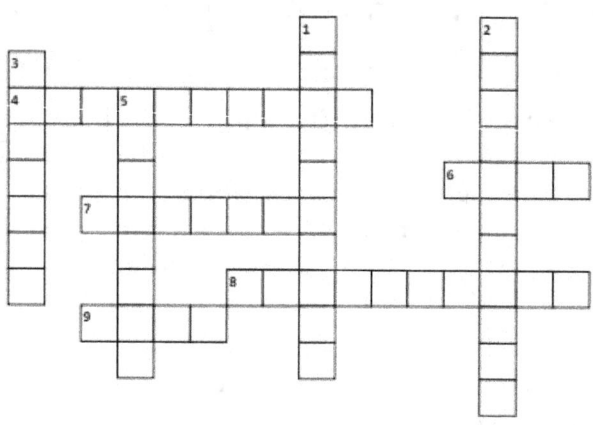

Across
4. I co-ruled with Thutmose III
6. I was a god. Hatshepsut said I was her father
7. Where Thutmose II won his 1st great victory
8. My astronomer invented the water clock
9. Hatshepsut sent an expedition here

Down
1. I married Hatshepsut when she was 12
2. I co-ruled with Hatshepsut until she died
3. I chased the Hyksos out of Egypt
5. I was Hatshepshut's Chief Minister & architect

Image source[40]

Chapter 7: Akhenaten: The Heretic

Akhenaten (1352-1334 BCE) broke the mold of what pharaohs were supposed to do. His real name was Amenhotep IV, but he changed it five years into his reign. His new name, Akhenaten, meant "effective for Aten." His name change represented a radical break in Egyptian religious beliefs. The Egyptian pharaoh was also the country's spiritual leader. Whatever he believed got imposed on everyone else. Akhenaten's goal was to reform Egyptian religion from the top down. Instead of worshiping many gods, he focused on only one: the Aten.

Did the ancient Egyptians always worship multiple gods? They may have been ***monotheistic*** (worshiping one god only) at the dawn of their civilization. Some scholars believe they only worshiped Amun, the creator, in their earliest days. Over time, they added more gods until they had dozens of primary deities and thousands of lesser gods. They happily followed this system for millennia.

And then, Akhenaten came onto the scene. By upending Egypt's religious system, he earned the title of *heretic*. A heretic believes and promotes things about religion that most people don't accept.

Who Might Have Influenced Akhenaten?

What happened in the seven decades between Thutmose III and Akhenaten? Were there any hints of religious change? Did other cultures influence Egypt's religion? The pharaohs married Nubian,

Syrian, Hurrian, and Babylonian princesses. These people were also polytheistic, yet they did influence the Egyptians. For instance, the people of Byblos worshiped the goddess Baalat Gebal. The Egyptians who traded with Byblos also worshiped this goddess and sent gifts to her temple. They associated her with their goddess Hathor.

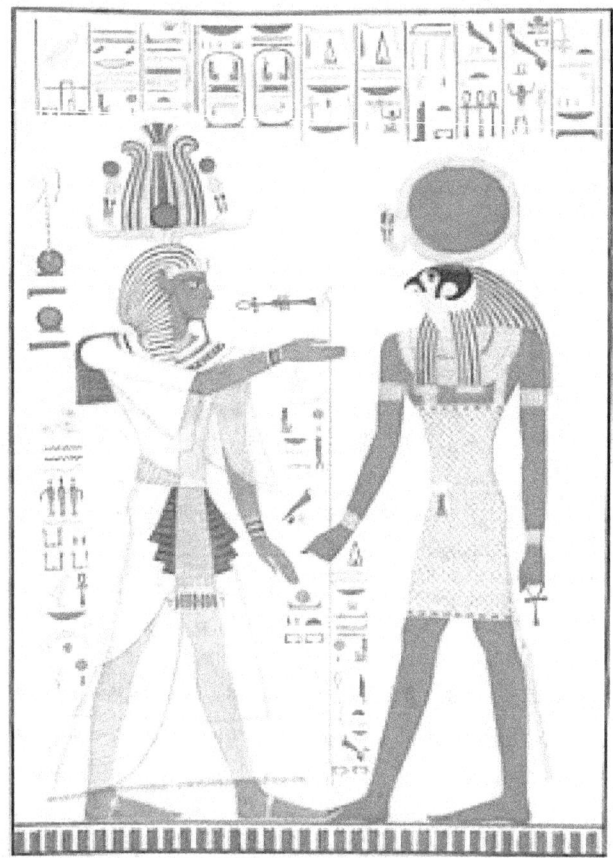

Pharaoh Merneptah and the sun god Ra [50]

The Israelites were the only known monotheistic people in the region. The first pharaoh to mention Israel in an inscription was the Nineteenth Dynasty Pharaoh Merneptah around 1208 BCE. On his victory monument, he bragged about clobbering the Hittites, Canaanites, Hurrians, and Israelites. The word he used for the Israelites was for a people, not a nation. Merneptah reigned when events in the Old Testament book of Judges unfolded. At that time, Israel was a loose confederation of twelve tribes living in Canaan, and they did not yet have a king.

Did Egyptian history say anything about the Israelites' exodus from Egypt, or was that just a myth? Obviously, such an event wouldn't have appeared on a victory monument. However, in the third century BCE, Egyptian priest and historian Manetho wrote about it. He said the exodus happened when Amenophis was king. Manetho wrote in Greek, and Amenophis was the Greek word for Amenhotep. Four pharaohs had this name in the Eighteenth Dynasty. Of the four pharaohs named Amenophis (Amenhotep), the one that may best fit the biblical timeline is Amenhotep II (1427–1400 BCE).

However, his story takes a radical turn from what Moses wrote in the Torah. The Egyptian spin on the story was that Amenophis wanted to rid Egypt of people with leprosy and other undesirables. He forced 80,000 of them to work in the quarries. The lepers asked a renegade priest named Osarseph to be their leader. He later changed his name to Moses. He told them not to worship the Egyptian gods. Manetho said the lepers formed a coalition with the Hyksos, who had fled Egypt hundreds of years earlier.

Amenophis couldn't fight the coalition, so he escaped to Ethiopia while the lepers and Hyksos wreaked havoc in Egypt. Oddly, instead of dying of leprosy, the undesirables grew to hundreds of thousands. Eventually, Amenophis built up support and came back to Egypt. He drowned some of the lepers in the sea and drove the rest into the Sinai Desert. These people eventually settled in Judea and became the Jews.

At any rate, Akhenaten knew about the Israelites and their religion. Of course, the Israelites weren't very good monotheists. They kept straying into polytheism. Nevertheless, they could have put some ideas into Akhenaten's mind.

Was Amenhotep II the pharaoh during the Exodus?[81]

How Did Akhenaten's Family Influence Him?

Akhenaten's family dynamics became increasingly bizarre as he grew up. His father, Amenhotep III, became pharaoh as a child. He immediately married Tiye, his Great Royal Wife. Tiye was Akhenaten's mother, and she had several other children. She had unusual power for an Egyptian queen and helped her husband run the country. Artwork shows her as the same height as her husband, indicating they were equal partners in the marriage.

Amenhotep III also married two Babylonian princesses and the Hurrian princess Gilukhepa. Later, he married Gilukhepa's niece, Tadukhipa. Yet, he refused to give any of his daughters as brides to foreign kings. He didn't want foreigners to claim Egypt's throne via marriage. As Amenhotep III got older, things got really weird. He married two of his daughters and made them Great Royal Wives. Amenhotep III was the first pharaoh known to marry his children.

Like Hatshepsut, Amenhotep III claimed the god Amun was his biological father. The worship of Amun was quite popular at this time. The priests of Amun had almost equal standing with the royal family. By the time Akhenaten became pharaoh, the priests of Amun owned more land than he did.

Amenhotep III became increasingly interested in the Aten-tjehen, or the "Dazzling Sun Disk." (The Aten was the Sun Disk, or the visible sun—an aspect of the sun god Ra.) He promoted the solar cult—the worship of the sun—and even took the title "Sun Disk" for himself. Yet, he didn't worship the sun god exclusively. He also encouraged the worship of the moon, specifically the moon god Nebmaatre of Soleb, adopted from the Nubians. He believed that he was the moon god's living image on earth. In a sense, he thought he was the sun and the moon.

Akhenaten became pharaoh around 1352 BCE when his father died. He had a distinctive appearance. His face was long and thin, with high cheekbones, full lips, and an exceptionally pointed chin. Akhenaten's wife was the beautiful and elegant Nefertiti. They had six daughters together but no sons. Akhenaten had another wife named Kiya. This marriage was probably a love match, as an inscription called her "the king's greatly beloved wife."

Akhenaten (Amenhotep III)[a]

He also married his full sister, "The Younger Lady" (the name given to her mummy in recent years). Although it's unclear which sister she was, DNA analysis of her mummy shows she was the daughter of Amenhotep III and Tiye. It also proved she was the mother of the famous King Tutankhamun. Her mummy shows she shared her brother's unusual facial characteristics, including the long, pointy chin. She suffered a terrible wound that crushed her left cheek and jaw and killed her. Was it accidental, such as a kick from a horse, or was she the victim of violence, like from an axe blow? If so, who murdered her and why? We may never know.

How Did Akhenaten Focus on the Aten?

As we mentioned, Akhenaten's father had worshiped the Aten, but Akhenaten took it to the next level. At first, Akhenaten devoted his personal worship to the Aten but acknowledged that other gods existed and could be worshiped. Things began to change in the eighth year of his reign. By then, he had already changed his name from Amenhotep to Akhenaten.

Akhenaten next claimed to be the only human who could know and connect with the god. He said that the Aten was the only god who could be officially worshiped; however, no one except for him could worship the Aten. Everyone else had to worship Akhenaten as the Aten's living incarnation. He banned idols of any other gods and shut down the state temples of other deities. He even erased the name of Amun from Egypt's monuments. By suppressing Amun's worship, he reined in the power of Amun's priests, a threat to his kingship.

Akhenaten worships the Aten, portrayed as the sun's rays.[58]

The only image Akhenaten allowed was the sun with its rays. He taught that the image was only a representation of the Aten. No one could truly understand or portray the god. In Akhenaten's hymns and inscriptions, he spoke of the Aten as the supreme god. This loving and all-powerful creator maintained the universe. Egypt's priests had worshiped other gods in dark temples, but Akhenaten took worship outside, into the bright sunshine.

Why Did He Build a New Capital City?

When Akhenaten changed his name, he also built a new capital named after his god. Akhetaten meant "Horizon of the Aten." It was on the eastern side of the Nile River, about 250 miles north of the previous capital of Thebes. A break in the cliffs directly east of the city let in the first rays of the rising sun, bathing the city in its light and warmth. Today, it is called Amarna. No earlier city had existed on this site, as Akhenaten wanted his new city to have no former temples to any other god. The new capital represented a break from the old Egyptian gods and especially the priests of Amun. He wanted his capital to be completely dedicated to the Aten.

The new city was planned and built remarkably quickly, thanks to efficient new methods. The builders used smaller limestone blocks of standard size. Workers used mudbrick for many buildings; they could make the bricks quickly and then whitewash them. The city was ready for the royal family to move in within about three years. While workers built it, Akhenaten ordered new temples to the Aten built in Egypt's major cities, like Heliopolis and Memphis.

A magnificent open-air temple to the Aten stood in Akhetaten's center. The grand royal palace in the north overlooked the Nile. The entire city covered about eight miles, with land on the other side of the Nile used for farming.

Akhenaten built Akhetaten to honor his one god, yet the ordinary people weren't fans of monotheism. Archaeologists have dug up small idols in Akhetaten, like the hippopotamus goddess of childbirth. People only lived in Akhetaten for a few decades. After Akhenaten died, King Tutankhamun made Thebes the capital again. Akhetaten quickly became a ghost city covered by sand until a Jesuit priest rediscovered it in the 1700s CE.

Bust of Akhenaten[54]

In the late 1800s CE, the **_Amarna letters_** were found in the city's ruins. These were a collection of clay tablets with the cuneiform writing used in the ancient Middle East. Although Egypt used papyrus for writing, the West Asians inscribed their writing on damp clay, which hardened into tablets. The nice thing about these tablets is that some lasted for thousands of years and left a historical record. The kings of Syria, Babylonia, Egypt, and other nations exchanged letters regularly. These letters found in the long-abandoned city opened a window into the relationships between the royalty of Egypt and West Asia.

The kings called each other brothers, sent gifts to each other, and planned the royal weddings of their children. They asked each other for help when needed, such as during an invasion or famine. When they had medical problems, one king would send the other his favorite doctor, medicine, or magician.

Sometimes, they wrote to complain. For instance, the Babylonian king Burna-Buriash II wrote to Akhenaten, "I was ill, and you never wrote me a get-well note!" His next grievance was far worse. Egypt controlled Canaan at the time, but the Babylonian merchants passing through Canaan to Egypt were being attacked. "You need to execute those bandits and pay me back for the money they stole!"

In Akhenaten's day, there were four "great powers" of the Middle East. They were the Egyptians, Babylonians, Hurrians, and Hittites. All four kingdoms wanted control of Syria, an important trade crossroads. The Hittite kingdom was between the Black Sea and the Mediterranean in western Turkey. When Akhenaten was busy building Akhetaten, the Hittites snatched Egypt's territory in Syria. For the rest of the Eighteenth Dynasty, the Egyptians and the Hittites were at each other's throats.

Did Akhenaten's Wife Nefertiti Co-Reign with Him?

Nefertiti was Akhenaten's Great Royal Wife, but was she more? Artwork shows her riding in a chariot. Two carvings show her with her hand raised, holding a weapon, about to violently strike an enemy. Another time, she is trampling the enemy. It's unlikely she actually went to war, so the artwork must be symbolic.

An iconic scene in ancient Egyptian art shows an Egyptian king holding a kneeling prisoner by the hair. The king holds a mace or some other weapon in the air, about to strike. This scene is repeated over and over throughout ancient Egypt's history. Some scholars suggest the scene doesn't always represent an actual event. It might show the continued power of the Egyptian monarch over the enemy.

This scene was always used for kings. Placing Queen Nefertiti in this scene is a vital clue that she became a co-pharaoh with her husband. Some historians believe that Akhenaten made her his co-pharaoh a few years before he died. Nefertiti's name disappeared from royal inscriptions in Akhenaten's twelfth year as king. Did she die, or did she get a promotion?

Nefertiti[55]

After Nefertiti "disappeared," Akhenaten suddenly had a co-pharaoh. The co-pharaoh's name was Neferneferuaten. She had the title "Akhet-en-hyes," which meant "effective for her husband." That must have meant this pharaoh was a woman and one of Akhenaten's wives. Neferneferuaten was almost certainly Nefertiti. She continued ruling for a year or two after Akhenaten died.

Roundup Activity: Two Truths and a Lie

Circle which of the three statements is <u>not</u> true. Check your answer in the back of the book.

- Akhenaten's wife was Nefertiti.
- Akhenaten promoted the worship of the moon god.
- Akhenaten built a new city devoted to the Aten.

Chapter 8: Tutankhamun: A Boy and His Legacy

If you asked someone to name an Egyptian pharaoh, chances are they'd say "King Tut!" A few might say Ramesses. Most people would not know the names of the other Egyptian kings unless they're addicted to the History Channel. What made Tutankhamun, who ruled from 1332 to 1323 BCE, so famous? What did he accomplish as Egypt's king?

The truth is that he didn't achieve nearly as much as some of the more obscure kings. After all, he was only eight or nine years old when he became pharaoh, and he died when he was only eighteen or nineteen. A regent ran Egypt for most of his reign. Yes, he (and his regent) accomplished significant changes in Egyptian culture. But Tutankhamun is more famous for his mummy than what he did while living.

What Was His Childhood Like?

Tut's father was Akhenaten, and his mother was one of Akhenaten's full sisters. This meant he only had one set of grandparents: Amenhotep III and Queen Tiye. Although DNA analysis reveals Tut's mother was his father's sister, it doesn't tell us which sister. Tiye had four or five daughters. When Tut was born, Akhenaten, the religious revolutionary, named him Tutankhaten, which meant "the living image of Aten," or "the life of Aten is perfect."

Tutankhaten was born toward the end of his father's reign when his stepmother Nefertiti was likely co-pharaoh. He had a wet nurse named

Maia. (Maia had her own baby but also breastfed Tutankhaten.) A carving of Tut as a teen shows him with Maia in an endearing scene. One of Maia's titles was "educator," which means she was also likely his tutor. She was also called "great one of the harem." Maia was probably a relative of Tutankhaten.

Tutankhamun and Maia[56]

Tutankhaten's birth mother must have died before he became pharaoh. No mention of her in his reign has been found. Typically, a pharaoh's mother appeared in artwork with her son and was a key influence. The fatal blow to her face, if murder, may have happened in the chaos surrounding Akhenaten's death. Her royal lineage and position as Akhenaten's wife made her a strong contender to the throne, a threat to Nefertiti and her son-in-law, Smenkhkare.

Tutankhaten was about seven when his father, Akhenaten, died. Two shadowy figures ruled Egypt for the next two years. One was Neferneferuaten, probably Nefertiti. The other was the mysterious Smenkhkare. His wife was Meritaten, a daughter of Akhenaten and Nefertiti. Smenkhkare may have been the son of Akhenaten's brother, Thutmose, who was the crown prince until his early death. Smenkhkare probably died after only ruling for a year.

This couple is probably Smenkhkare and his wife Meritaten.[57]

Rise to Throne and Name Change

Either Neferneferuaten and Smenkhkare died, or Tutankhaten and his supporters grew strong enough to overthrow them. King Tut's reign marked the return to Egypt's polytheistic religion, with Amun the chief god again. Around age twelve, Tutankhaten took the new name of Tutankhamun, "living image of Amun." However, he still reverenced the Aten. He married his half-sister, the daughter of Akhenaten and Nefertiti. She was born Ankhesenpaaten, meaning "she lives for Aten." When Tut changed his name, she changed hers to Ankhesenamun, "she lives for Amun." Although they adopted Egypt's polytheism, they still reverenced the Aten, as a painting shows the couple bathed in the sun's rays.

Tutankhamun and his wife, Ankhesenamun[58]

Ankhesenamun was apparently Tutankhamun's only wife. The couple had no surviving children, but Ankhesenamun got pregnant at least twice. One female child died in the second trimester of pregnancy, and the other girl died shortly after she was born. Both girls were mummified and buried with their father.

Tutankhamun was too young to rule on his own, so who was his regent? His mother was probably dead by this time. The power behind the throne was Ay, whose wife Tey had been Nefertiti's wet nurse. During Akhenaten's reign, Ay was the overseer of the royal chariot horses. Ay and Horemheb, general of the armies, served as Tut's two closest advisors. Tutankhamun had a hot temper, and Horemheb wrote that he could calm the young king when he flew off the handle.

King Tutankhamun, the boy king[59]

Was Tutankhamun Physically Disabled?

Did Tutankhamun inherit any genetic defects from his parents' incestuous marriage? Remarkably, Tut didn't have the extremely long chin that both his mother and father had. However, an analysis of his mummy leads some scholars to say he was frail and deformed. In his tomb were 130 walking sticks, which some interpret to mean he couldn't walk on his own. His mummy appears to have a club foot or a foot that was twisted and turned in.

However, several Egyptologists and physicians point out that mummification could have caused the apparent club foot. They have seen other mummies whose tight wrappings have distorted the foot's shape. If King Tut had a club foot, the long bones in his leg would have shown signs of wear and distress, yet they were perfectly aligned. Moreover, the sandals in his

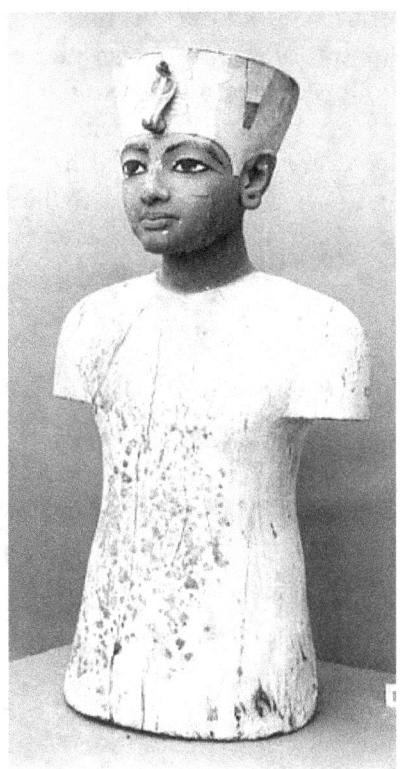

A wooden figure of King Tut[60]

tomb did not show uneven wear. (Of course, they might have been a new pair). Scholars think the walking sticks were a status symbol, not an aid for walking.

What Did He Do as King?

Tutankhamun and his advisors restored the old polytheistic system in Egypt. During Tut's father's reign, the temples had fallen into ruin. The priests moaned that such neglect irritated the gods. "If we ask a god or goddess for advice, they won't listen!" King Tut rebuilt or restored the old temples and even built massive new temples.

About four years into his reign, when he would have been twelve or thirteen, his court left Akhetaten and moved to Memphis. The earlier kings of the Eighteenth Dynasty had ruled from Thebes, and it continued as Egypt's religious center. Yet, Memphis had a history as Egypt's capital stretching back to the Old Kingdom.

King Tutankhamun had to contend with the economic crisis that his father left behind. Akhenaten was so laser-focused on promoting the worship of the Aten that he ignored Egypt's foreign relations. The trade routes crumbled because bandits ran rampant. Tutankhamun worked to restore relationships with Egypt's old allies, like the Hurrians and Babylonians. Tut warred in Nubia, Canaan, and Syria, gaining back lost territory. Whether he actually led his armies is questionable. He would have been too young for most of his reign.

Tutankhamun as a sphinx, trampling the enemy[81]

How Did King Tut Die?

Tutankhamun died in his late teens. The cause of his death is a topic of fierce debate among Egyptologists. Some believe he might have died from a disability; however, it is doubtful that he was severely disabled. He did have a broken left thigh bone, which some scholars think might have happened in a chariot crash. The broken bone may have gotten infected (osteomyelitis). If untreated (and no one had antibiotics, then), osteomyelitis kills 20 percent of the people who have it.

King Tut's DNA indicated he had been sick multiple times with several strains of malaria. One strain of the mosquito-borne illness he had was Plasmodium falciparum, the most severe type of malaria that is often fatal. Malaria causes chills, fever, and headache, but the worst strain causes breathing issues, confusion, seizures, and coma. Even today, it kills over 400,000 people a year.

Another potential cause of death is an epidemic. The Egyptian military stationed in Syria had the bubonic plague or tularemia (rabbit fever) not long after Tutankhamun died. Both diseases are bacterial and have a 50 percent death rate without antibiotics.

Who Ruled after Tutankhamun Died?

Tutankhamun's death ended the Eighteenth Dynasty. Tut's advisor, Ay, became the next pharaoh and ruled from around 1323 to 1319 BCE. He oversaw Tutankhamun's funeral. Oddly, he even conducted the "Opening of the Mouth" ceremony. Usually, an important priest did this. Ay wore a leopard skin during the ceremony, which the high priest typically wore. Of course, the embalming process took seventy days. Ay would have been installed as pharaoh by the time the funeral took place, giving him priestly status.

Ay at Tutankhamun's funeral[62]

Tut's Queen and the Hittite Prince

Tutankhamun's wife, Ankhesenamun, found herself in an awkward position when her teenage husband suddenly died. Ay had taken the throne. He had some royal connections but no valid claim to the throne other than serving as Tutankhamun's advisor. He tried to fix the problem by forcing a marriage with Ankhesenamun. Not only was she Tut's wife, but she was also the daughter of Akhenaten and Nefertiti.

Ankhesenamun looked down her nose at the older man. She was far too royal to marry him! She could rule Egypt herself if she could find a royal husband. But who? In desperation, she wrote to Suppiluliuma I, the Hittite king: "My husband died, and I have no sons. I hear you have many sons. Could you send one of your sons to be my husband? They are trying to force me to marry a servant!"

Suppiluliuma was stunned when he received her letter. The Egyptians never allowed marriages of their royal women to foreign princes. Furthermore, royal women never negotiated their marriages. "I've never heard of such a thing!" Suppiluliuma gasped.

Yet, why not marry one of his sons to the Egyptian queen? His son could become Egypt's pharaoh. Suppiluliuma wondered if the letter was legitimate. He sent his chief advisor to Egypt to determine if the situation was as she described. The advisor returned with a second letter from the queen.

"Why do you doubt me? If what I said wasn't true, why would I send such shameful news to a foreign land? It's all still true. My husband died. I have no son. I refuse to marry a servant. I haven't written any other country, only to you! Send me one of your sons to be my husband, and he will be king of Egypt."

Finally, Suppiluliuma sent his son, Zannanza, to marry the Egyptian queen. But Ay must have gotten wind that he was coming because someone killed Zannanza before he arrived at the Egyptian queen's palace. Suppiluliuma was livid. He ordered his armies to attack the Egyptian lands in Syria and Canaan.

Suppiluliuma I, Hittite King from 1370-1330 BCE[68]

The Hittites pulverized the Egyptians and brought hundreds of captives back to their land of Hatti. But Suppiluliuma didn't know that the plague was circulating around Syria. The captive Egyptian soldiers brought the plague with them to the Hittites, killing Suppiluliuma and his crown prince Arnuwanda and wiping out the Hittite military.

Horemheb Erases Tutankhamun

Horemheb ruled from 1319 to 1292 BCE. Although not royal, he had worked his way to power as the commander-in-chief of Egypt's army. King Tut sent him on diplomatic missions and made him his crown prince before he died. However, when Tutankhamun died, Horemheb was in Syria fighting the Hittites (and the plague). Taking advantage of his absence, Ay somehow elbowed his way into becoming the next pharaoh. Horemheb sat back and waited. Ay was elderly and probably wouldn't live long.

When Ay died four years later, Horemheb got his revenge. He shattered Ay's sarcophagus and erased his name and portraits from his tomb. He then wiped out the memory of Akhenaten, the heretic. Akhenaten had offended the gods and disrupted Egypt's harmony. Horemheb struck his name off royal documents and kings' lists. He flattened the city of Akhetaten and chiseled off Akhenaten's name from monuments throughout Egypt.

Horemheb continued his quest to rewrite history, erasing Neferneferuaten and Smenkhkare. After all, they were connected to Akhenaten. He even erased Tutankhamun, although the boy had named him his crown prince. However, Horemheb did not disturb Tutankhamun's tomb. Like Hatshepsut, Akhenaten and Tutankhamun became the forgotten pharaohs.

Discovery of Tut's Tomb by Howard Carter

In 1907 CE, Lord Carnarvon of Highclere Castle (where Downton Abbey was filmed) financed Howard Carter's quest to find King Tutankhamun's tomb. The forgotten king's existence had come to light when Akhetaten was unearthed at Amarna. After World War I interrupted his search for several years, Carter renewed his search in 1917. However, he found nothing, and Lord Carnarvon threatened to cut off his funding.

Carter returned to the Valley of the Kings, where a series of tombs had been carved into the hills. In November 1922, he removed debris in front of a large tomb. A boy bringing water to his workers tripped over a stone, but it wasn't just a random rock. It was a flight of steps leading underground to a doorway. Exhilarated, Carter telegrammed Lord Carnarvon. When Carnarvon arrived two weeks later, Carter chiseled a hole into the top of the door. He held a candle to the opening and peered inside.

"Can you see anything?"

"Yes! Wonderful things!"

King Tutankhamun's death mask[64]

Once they opened the tomb, they confirmed it belonged to King Tutankhamun. Instead of being carved into the hillside, like the surrounding tombs, it was cut into the valley floor. No one expected it to be there, including tomb robbers over the millennia. The tomb had been mostly untouched. Water had seeped in and damaged some of the items inside. Yet, unlike any other royal tomb in the Valley of the Kings, most of its treasures were undisturbed.

King Tutankhamun's mummy lay in a coffin nested inside two larger coffins. Covering his face was the spectacular gold death mask that has become iconic. It was solid gold inlaid with gemstones and weighed almost twenty-three pounds. A magic spell had been inscribed on the back of the mask to guide the king safely to the underworld. Thousands of other objects lay in the tomb, including a gilded throne, statues of King Tut, chariots, an alabaster lotus-shaped drinking vessel, furniture, baskets of fruit and meat, clothing, and cosmetics. Touchingly, King Tut's childhood toys had been buried with him.

What Myths Swirled Regarding His Tomb?

Newspaper headlines in 1922 announced a curse found at the entrance to Tutankhamun's tomb: "They who enter this sacred tomb shall be swiftly visited by the wings of death!" It turned out that this lurid inscription wasn't from ancient times. Neither was it on Tut's tomb. The journalists made it up to sell papers! Nevertheless, Lord Carnarvon died within months of blood poisoning, and the rumors resurfaced. Other team members mysteriously died, leaving some convinced that the tomb was cursed.

A shabti doll buried with Tut[65]

What Legacy Did King Tut Leave Behind?

Horemheb thought he had erased the memory of Akhenaten and Tutankhamun. However, the discovery of Akhetaten at Amarna shed light on Akhenaten's role as a religious revolutionary. Tutankhamun died as a teenager before workers completed his royal tomb. Consequently, he was buried in a borrowed tomb. His chief advisor, Ay, buried Tutankhamun in the tomb he had prepared for himself. Later, after serving as pharaoh, Ay was buried in the tomb meant for Tutankhamun.

The small, modest tomb where Tutankhamun lay escaped the attention of tomb robbers. After all, if no one knew he existed, why even look for his tomb?

King Tutankhamun's greatest legacy was the astounding treasures and records hidden with him for thousands of years. Although relatively insignificant as a pharaoh, Tutankhamun is the most well-known. Why? His tomb was opened in the modern day of newspapers and magazines. "Tutmania," the sensational news and photos of this astonishing find, circled the globe and continues to capture the imagination.

Roundup Activity: "Who Am I" Word Search

Find the answer to the questions below in the puzzle going up, down, forward, backward, and diagonally. Check your answers in the back of the book.

A	N	K	H	E	S	E	N	A	M	U	N	R
M	A	I	A	Q	P	O	N	M	L	K	O	J
E	I	H	G	F	E	D	C	B	A	E	V	M
N	E	T	A	N	E	H	K	A	Y	B	R	T
H	O	R	E	M	H	E	B	E	U	B	A	R
O	D	E	H	T	A	F	E	H	T	O	N	T
T	S	E	C	M	O	C	N	B	A	M	R	O
E	R	A	K	H	K	N	E	M	S	N	A	T
P	A	H	G	I	L	Y	E	H	T	D	C	N
I	A	H	T	U	I	R	T	E	H	T	D	N
I	A	Y	A	T	W	E	H	T	M	A	Y	I
I	S	U	P	P	I	L	U	L	I	U	M	A

1. I was King Tut's grandfather
2. I was King Tut's grandmother
3. I was Tut's father, the religious revolutionary
4. I was Tut's wet nurse and tutor
5. Neferneferuaten and I ruled Egypt just before King Tut
6. This was my new name after King Tut and I got married
7. I was King Tut's regent and the pharaoh after him

8. I was the Hittite king who died of the plague after capturing Egyptian soldiers
9. I became king after Ay and erased King Tut and his father from the records
10. I was the lord who financed Howard Carter's discovery of Tut's tomb

Chapter 9: The Battle of Kadesh

"He's coming! Ramesses is on his way! I saw a cloud of dust down in the valley," the shepherd reported, running down the mountain to join his companions.

"Iasmakh! Ride quickly to Kadesh. Let Muwatalli know they're approaching."

Iasmakh jumped on his horse and disappeared over a hill. Meanwhile, the other two shepherds moved under a tree near the road. When Pharaoh Ramesses II rode up with his hundreds of chariots, he saw an idyllic scene. Sheep and goats peacefully grazed on the hillside. Two shepherds were sipping goat milk in the shade by the Orontes River.

Ramesses reined his horses to a stop as his men breathed a sigh of relief. They had been riding for hours. The king stepped out of his chariot and nodded to his interpreter. They approached the shepherds, who stood up and bowed.

"Sire! Please! Sit down and rest here in the shade. You must be exhausted! Have some goat milk with honey."

"Thank you," Ramesses said, smiling. "But I won't rest until I reach Kadesh. How far is it?"

"Not far. A two-hour march."

"Where are Muwatalli and the Hittites?"

"Oh, they're nowhere near here!" the shepherds assured Ramesses. "King Muwatalli heard you were coming and fled to Aleppo. He's rounding up reinforcements. They say he was trembling with fear when he heard your army was on the way."

Ramesses grinned. "As he ought to be!"

The Egyptian commander-in-chief approached Ramesses. "Sire, the horses need water. And the foot soldiers need time to catch up."

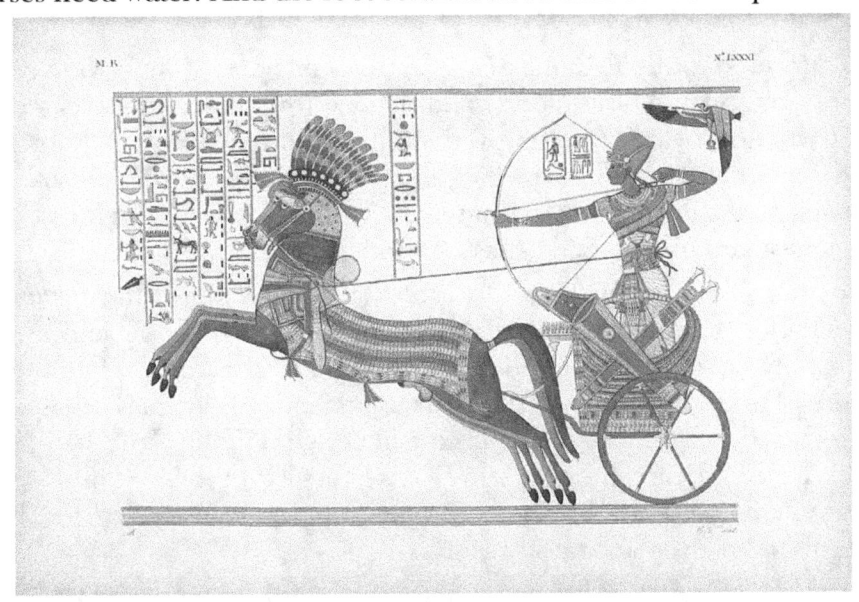

Ramesses stands in his two-horse chariot with the reins tied around his waist so he can fire an arrow.⁶⁶

"Right. There's water here for the horses and men. We'll let everyone drink, then march on to Kadesh."

"With just the first unit? That's only 500 chariots and about 5,000 men! The other three units and chariots are far behind."

"Muwatalli's in Aleppo. He probably only left a small force in Kadesh. We'll ride ahead and set things straight in Kadesh. We need to reinstall our military there, or Muwatalli will retake the city when he gets reinforcements. The other units will catch up soon. We'll all spend the night at Kadesh."

Ramesses didn't know that Muwatalli had bribed the shepherds to give the Egyptians misinformation and keep him informed of their movement. The Hittites had *not* left the area and far outnumbered Ramesses's troops.

The 1274 BCE Battle of Kadesh (Qadesh) in Syria was one of the most significant military conflicts in ancient Egyptian history. What was the background behind this battle? Why were the Egyptians and Hittites fighting? What made Kadesh so pivotal? How did Ramesses almost get killed in the struggle, and who won? Let's jump into the thrilling story to discover what happened.

What Led Up to the Battle?

After Horemheb died, Ramesses I founded ancient Egypt's Nineteenth Dynasty, although he was elderly and reigned for less than two years. His family was not royal but had proved themselves in the military. Ramesses I had served as Horemheb's chief advisor. Because Horemheb had no surviving sons, he appointed Ramesses as his successor. Ramesses, in turn, appointed his son Seti as his crown prince.

For two centuries leading up to the Battle of Kadesh, the Egyptians and Hittites fought an on-again-off-again war. Syria, Lebanon, and Canaan lay between Egypt and Hatti, the Hittite kingdom. (Hatti was in western Turkey, around where Ankara is today.) Egypt had loosely controlled Canaan from early times, although Hittite clans had lived there from at least the Middle Kingdom. Egypt had robust trade arrangements with the city-states in Syria and Lebanon. It even held political power over several city-states.

During his reign, Akhenaten had given little attention to foreign affairs, and the Hittites had swarmed into Syria and Lebanon. Ramesses I sent his son Seti off to Canaan and Syria to take back the land Egypt had lost in the chaotic past half-century.

Seti I⁸⁷

Seti I fought fiercely against the Hittites and recouped most of the lost territory in Canaan and Lebanon. After he conquered Lebanon, its chiefs sent yearly tribute of cedar wood. Seti also fought against a Libyan invasion of Egypt and subdued a rebellion in Nubia. When his father died, Seti ruled Egypt from around 1290 to 1279 BCE. He established military forts on the "Ways of Horus," a coastal road running through Gaza. He temporarily got control of Kadesh and the surrounding Amorite territory. However, it was so close to the Hittite kingdom that he could not hold it.

Meanwhile, Muwatalli II, the grandson of Suppiluliuma I, had become king of the Hittites. They were recovering from a fifty-year setback from the plague. Before getting struck down by the plague, Suppiluliuma I's goal was to control all of Syria west of the Euphrates.

The westernmost region of Turkey, on the coast of the Aegean Sea, was the land of Arzawa. Muwatalli's empire included Arzawa during his reign. Wilusa was a key city in Arzawa, and it paid tribute to the Hittites. Located on Turkey's northwestern coast, Wilusa was probably ancient Troy. Once thought to be mythological, scholars now believe Troy was a real place, based on Hittite records and archaeological finds at Wilusa. The Trojan War probably happened about seventy years after the Battle of Kadesh.

Sculpture of a young Ramesses II[88]

While Muwatalli grew in power, Seti I died, and his son, Ramesses II, became Egypt's pharaoh. He was the most commanding and dynamic of the New Kingdom pharaohs. Ramesses II became pharaoh when he was in his early twenties and ruled until he was in his nineties. He had many wives and around 100 children.

One of Ramesses II's first acts as pharaoh was pouncing on the infamous Sherden, one of the Sea Peoples. These were pirates who preyed on the ships sailing in the eastern Mediterranean Sea. No one is quite sure where the Sea Peoples came from. When Ramesses wrote about them, he didn't mention their homeland, almost as if he presumed everyone knew. However, he said they were in the league with the Hittites. Ramesses seemed to appreciate their fighting ability. Whenever he defeated a group of the Sea Peoples, he drafted them into his military.

Ramesses II, with his military under him[69]

What Were the Hittites and Egyptians Fighting Over?

The Hittites and Egyptians had competing interests in Syria, which lay on the Fertile Crescent's upper curve. The Fertile Crescent was an upside-down U-shaped trade highway with Syria as its pivotal center. From Syria, merchants followed the Euphrates River southeast through Assyria and Babylonia. They could also travel south through Lebanon and Canaan to Egypt or northwest to the Hittite region of Hatti and on to the fabulously wealthy Troy. Syria was a place where cultures mixed and mingled, one of the ancient world's most strategic trade hubs. It's no wonder that so many empires wanted control of Syria.

Fertile Crescent[70]

Syria had been on ancient Egypt's northern border for much of its history. Canaan had been a sort of buffer zone, protecting Egypt from invasions from the Assyrians, Mitanni, and other powerful nations. Kadesh lay near the border between Lebanon and Syria. It was on the Orontes River, which connected some of ancient Syria's major cities, like Homs and Hama.

The Hittites had taken control of Kadesh, and Ramesses II was determined to get it back.

What Weapons and Military Men Did Each Side Have?

The Egyptians had about 20,000 men, but the Hittites had around 37,000. Muwatalli had convinced nineteen city-states in Syria and Turkey to join his side. The Hittite chariots numbered around 3,000, while the Egyptians had 2,000. With about 5,000 chariots altogether, it was the largest chariot battle in history.

The Hittites had been one of the earliest civilizations to use horse-drawn chariots with two spoked wheels. They had learned the skill of training chariot horses from the Hurrians. The Hittites had been riding chariots into battle for almost 400 years, far longer than the Egyptians.

Hittite three-man, two-horse war chariot[71]

However, the Hittite chariots were heavier than the Egyptian chariots and held three men. One man was the driver, one carried a large shield to deflect arrows, and the third shot arrows or flung his spear at the enemy. The axle of the Hittite chariot was usually in the middle, allowing it to carry the extra weight of three men.

This made the Hittite chariots slower and clumsier than the Egyptian chariots. They used their chariots like battering rams, charging into lines of foot soldiers, crushing them and breaking their formation.

The Egyptians generally had two men in their chariots: a driver and an archer. Egyptian art typically showed the pharaoh in the chariot by himself with the reins tied around his waist. Egyptian chariots were mostly wood and lightweight. The axle was at the rear of the chariot, allowing for astounding maneuverability even at high speed. The men stood on a mesh of woven leather straps, which was lightweight and easier to balance when hitting bumps. The primary function of Egyptian chariots in battle was as moving platforms for shooting arrows or chasing down and trampling the enemy.

The Hittites were ahead of their day by using iron weapons. They had been smelting iron ore since 1400 BCE near the border of Syria. Their iron weapons were slightly harder and less likely to break than the bronze weapons used by the Egyptians. Even better, iron was cheap. It was readily available in Turkey and Syria. The Hittites could afford to outfit their entire army with iron weapons. The primary Hittite weapons were long spears, short daggers, and long, thin swords.

The Egyptians didn't have iron for another half-century. As mentioned, some of their weapons were bronze, an alloy of copper and tin. Copper was readily available in the Sinai Desert and along the Red Sea. But tin was more challenging to get and not readily available. The expense and rarity of tin made bronze weapons more expensive. Only the elite soldiers could carry them. Everyone else had to use copper, which was more brittle than iron and hard to sharpen.

In one image of Ramesses with his military, some soldiers carried long, pointed swords and round shields. These were the Sherden, the Sea People drafted by Ramesses II. He used them as his bodyguards in the Battle of Kadesh. In the painting, the Sherden wore longer skirts and distinctive helmets with horns and a ball at the top. Ramesses's Egyptian spearmen carried large, rectangular shields. No one seemed to wear body armor, except possibly some quilting in the chest area. Everyone wore sandals.

Ramesses II's soldiers[72]

What Happened in the Battle?

Ramesses II was so eager to capture Kadesh that he surged ahead with the Amun unit of his army, leaving the other three units far behind. They crossed the Orontes River and set up camp near Kadesh. But then, Ramesses received horrifying news. His scouts had captured two Hittite soldiers who were spying on the Egyptians. When Ramesses interrogated them, they told him, "Muwatalli is here! And he has more men than sand on the beach."

Ramesses whipped around and ordered several charioteers to race to the other divisions. "Tell them to come at full speed!"

He looked up and smiled to see his Ra division fording the river and working their way up the slope to his Amun division. But the Hittite army suddenly appeared from behind a small mountain. They charged the Ra division with their chariots, scattering them in all directions.

Ramesses wrote his version of how the battle went down in the Poem of Pentaur and other inscriptions. The Hittites confronted him with 37,000 troops and 3,000 chariots. With the Amun and Ra divisions, Ramesses only had about 10,000 men and 1,000 chariots. He was outnumbered more than three to one. And yet, despite his youthfulness, Ramesses was a veteran warrior. He had gone to war with his father from age fourteen.

Ramesses raced down the slope in his chariot, leading his men in a charge against the Hittite chariots that were coming between his two units. But he got too far ahead of his men, and the Hittite chariots circled him, cutting him off. Fortunately, Ramesses knew how to put the superior speed and maneuverability of his Egyptian chariot into play. He charged the Hittite line, time and time again, finally breaking through their lines. He was so fast and agile that the Hittite chariots couldn't compete.

He rejoined his men, but they were desperately outnumbered. When hope was almost lost, Ramesses saw his third unit, the Ptah division, arriving. He slumped in relief, then rubbed his hands in glee at the unfolding scene. Some of the Hittites had stopped at the Egyptian camp to plunder what they could find, leaving them trapped between the two sections of the Egyptian army.

Ramesses II continued to lead the Amun division in charges against the Hittites. His commanders led the Ra and Ptah divisions. The Ne'arin division finally arrived, yet the Egyptians were still outnumbered, almost two to one. Nevertheless, their chariots' speed and agility won the day. Curiously, Muwatalli II had a reserve force inside Kadesh, but he never called them out to join the battle. He may have decided that protecting the city was more important.

The Egyptians forced the Hittites and their allies to the banks of the river. Some jumped in and tried to swim away from their attackers, yet many drowned.

Ramesses forces the Hittites into the river.[78]

Who Won?

The victor depends on who was telling the story. Ramesses II went home and plastered paintings and inscriptions everywhere. He bragged of his spectacular victory against all odds. However, Muwatalli pointed out that he failed to take the city of Kadesh, where the Hittites had a substantial force. Ramesses II had neither the advanced siege engines to break through the high, thick walls nor the time to lay siege. He was far from home. Muwatalli could scrape up more allies and attack again. The Battle of Kadesh essentially ended in a draw. Ramesses won the land battle, but Muwatalli kept Kadesh.

Years later, Hattusili III, Muwatalli's brother, called Ramesses II out when he kept bragging about winning the Battle of Kadesh. About a decade had passed, and Hattusili was now the king of the Hittites. He and Ramesses had a mostly friendly relationship, calling each other "brother." Ramesses sent a doctor to Hattusili with special herbs when he was ill.

Nevertheless, the relationship was occasionally strained. When his sister couldn't get pregnant, Hattusili again asked Ramesses for medical help. Ramesses scoffed, "She's over fifty years old! It's not the gods' will for her to have children. If the gods change their minds, I'll immediately send a doctor and a magician to cure her."

The Peace Treaty

Despite random awkward exchanges, Hattusili III and Ramesses II were savvy enough to know that peace between Egypt and the Hittites was better for both nations. Fifteen years after the Battle of Kadesh, the two kings signed the "Eternal Treaty." This was the first peace treaty in history. Ramesses II promised that he would never attack the land of Hatti or try to steal any of its territory. Likewise, Hattusili III swore never to attack Egypt or take possession of its territory.

Roundup Activity: Draw a Soldier (or Two)

Draw a soldier in the Battle of Kadesh. He could be Egyptian or Hittite, or you could draw both in conflict with each other. You can decide if your soldier is a charioteer or a foot soldier. What will he wear? What weapons will he use? Review the photos in this chapter or find some online for ideas.

Chapter 10: The Fall of the New Kingdom

The Nineteenth Dynasty only lasted twenty-three years after Ramesses II died. What happened? This chapter will unwrap how this brilliant dynasty that restored Egypt's strength crashed and burned. The Twentieth Dynasty rose to power at the New Kingdom's final flowering. The priests of Amun gradually overpowered the pharaohs until they ruled Middle and Upper Egypt.

From this point until the Roman conquest, foreigners ruled Egypt. Libyan pharaohs controlled Egypt in the Third Intermediate Period. Then, Cyrus the Great conquered most of the Middle East. His Persian descendants triumphed over Egypt and ruled it for centuries. When Alexander the Great arrived in Egypt, the Egyptians cheered him as their rescuer from Persian oppression. Macedonian pharaohs governed Egypt for the next three centuries. The last pharaoh fell to the Romans in 30 BCE.

What Happened in the Later Years of the Nineteenth Dynasty?

The Nineteenth Dynasty was the epoch of Ramesses II. It lasted about a century, and Ramesses II was its pharaoh for two-thirds of that time. Egypt prospered economically and grew in power and size under his energetic rule. Ramesses wanted to sear the memory of his epic reign in history for all time. He built more monuments than any other pharaoh. He even inscribed his name and accomplishments on other pharaohs' monuments.

Ramesses built a new capital city called Pi-Ramesses only a mile from the ruins of the old Hyksos capital of Avaris on the easternmost branch of the Nile River. It was a strategic location. Avaris had been Egypt's wealthiest trade city, and the Nile Delta was Egypt's most affluent agricultural area. From Pi-Ramesses, the Nile flowed north fifty miles and emptied into the Mediterranean Sea. The city was not only Ramesses' capital but also his navy base. It was close enough for his navy and merchant ships to easily sail in and out of the Mediterranean, yet it was far enough inland to protect against surprise attacks from the sea.

Pi-Ramesses was breathtakingly beautiful and luxurious. During the annual flooding of the Nile, it was a city of islands linked by canals. Over 300,000 people lived in the bustling urban center. Nevertheless, Pi-Ramesses's prime location had a downside. By moving his capital away from Thebes, Ramesses no longer had close oversight of the priests of Amun at Thebes, who had threatened the power of pharaohs for centuries.

Ramesses built his new city with four major temples at its four corners. One was to Amun, Egypt's chief god. One was to Wadjet, the Nile Delta's ancient winged cobra goddess. The third temple was to Astarte, a West Asian goddess introduced by the Hyksos. The fourth temple was to Set, the chief god of the Hyksos, who connected him with Baal. Set was Egyptian but had a bad reputation as the god of chaos, foreigners, and storms. What's worse, he murdered his brother, Osiris, and chopped his body into pieces.

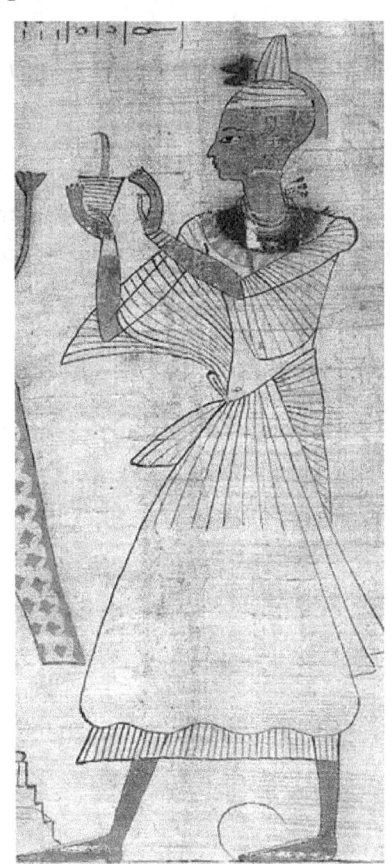

A priest of Amun[74]

Why did Ramesses elevate Set and Astarte? The famed Egyptologist Manfred Bietak believes that some Hyksos remained in the Delta region and continued to influence its culture. Ramesses had West Asian heritage through the intermarriage of his male ancestors with Syrian princesses. Analysis of his mummy's hair roots showed he was a natural redhead. His enthusiastic embrace of Hyksos and West Asian gods created tension with Amun's priests.

After Ramesses II died in his early nineties, the Nineteenth Dynasty fell into steep decline. Ramesses had around fifty sons, but his twelve oldest sons died before him. This left the elderly Merneptah as Egypt's new pharaoh.

Merneptah sent grain when the city-state of Ugarit in northern Syria suffered a famine. Later, Ugarit's king wrote Merneptah in a panic after seeing ships off his coast, probably the infamous Sea Peoples that Ramesses II had hired earlier. Whoever they were, they sacked Ugarit and stripped its vineyards and food stores. The Sea Peoples attacked Egypt again during Merneptah's reign. He said they sailed to Egypt from the "northern sea," most likely somewhere on the north Aegean or Black Sea. This time, they didn't come just to raid and plunder but to find somewhere to live. Merneptah said they brought their families and household goods, traveling not only by sea but over land by wagons.

Twosret, the last pharaoh of the Nineteenth Dynasty[78]

Infighting among Merneptah's descendants marked the rest of the Nineteenth Dynasty. Merneptah's daughter, Twosret (Tausret), was the last pharaoh of this dynasty. The historian Manetho said that Troy fell during Twosret's reign, which was around 1191-1189 BCE. After Twosret's death, Egypt fell into anarchy and civil war.

The Sea Peoples Reappear in the Twentieth Dynasty

A pharaoh named Setnakht took power and began the Twentieth Dynasty, the last of the New Kingdom. This dynasty lasted for a little over a century with ten pharaohs. Setnakht may have been a distant relative of the Ramesses family. All the pharaohs of the Twentieth Dynasty had the name Ramesses except him.

In 1180 BCE, when Setnakht's son, Ramesses III, was pharaoh, the Sea Peoples reappeared. This time, they utterly devastated the Hittites and the Amorite kingdom of Amurru in Lebanon. Ramesses III said their attack in Lebanon was so vicious and complete that it was like no one had ever lived there. The Sea Peoples went inland to Syria to attack Kadesh and Carchemish.

After this, the Sea Peoples traveled south by sea and land. At this time, Canaan was still under Egypt's control. (Egypt's borders extended up the Mediterranean coast to Lebanon.) Ramesses III's charioteers were waiting for them and killed everyone who dared cross into Canaan. Ramesses III sent his archers to guard the coast from Lebanon to Egypt. They hid along the shoreline, waiting for the Sea Peoples' ships to come ashore for water or to plunder food from nearby villages. In those days, sailors also beached their ships at night. When the Sea Peoples' ships approached land, the Egyptian archers unleashed volleys of flaming arrows at their vessels.

Nevertheless, some of the Sea Peoples' ships made it to Egypt and tried to sail into the Nile, where they met their doom. Hails of arrows from the Egyptian troops along the banks darkened the sky. The Egyptian navy rammed the Sea Peoples' ships, sinking them, and the bodies of the dead floated ashore.

After this annihilation, the Sea Peoples never again attacked Egypt. Yet, the Sea Peoples had shattered trade in the Mediterranean. This supply chain disruption was one cause of the Late Bronze Age collapse that shattered Greece and the Middle East.

What Contributed to the New Kingdom's Fall?

Ramesses III's reign ended when one of his lesser wives, Tiye, led a coup d'etat to make her son Pentawer king. The conspirators slit Ramesses's throat, killing him. His crown prince, Ramesses IV, overcame the attackers and sentenced them to death by burning. After this, the Twentieth Dynasty limped along for about eight decades. The Greek historian Diodorus Siculus wrote that its pharaohs were lazy, addicted to luxury, and did nothing of historical note.

Another factor was climate change, which led to cooler weather and less rainfall. The Nile did not flood as high as usual, leading to crop failure and famine. Riots erupted in protest of the lack of food and inept and corrupt leadership.

Meanwhile, the priests of Amun at Thebes asserted their power over Upper Egypt. They controlled the economy and most of the shipping trade. For the next few centuries, Egypt was divided into two or three kingdoms, with Amun's priests ruling most of the land.

How Did the Persian Empire Take Egypt?

In 525 BCE, the Persian king Cambyses II conquered Egypt using cats as a secret weapon. At first, the Egyptians had held the Persians off with their chariots, archers, and catapults. But then the Persians deployed cats. Why cats? The Egyptian war goddess Bastet had a cat's head and a woman's body. No one dared offend her, and anyone who killed a cat was executed.

The Persians painted Bastet's image on their shields and released hundreds of cats on their front lines. This tactic paralyzed the Egyptians. They didn't dare fire missiles at the Persians for fear of killing a cat or hitting Bastet's image. Unhinged, the Egyptians fled, and the Persians won the war. Egypt had never been part of another nation's empire. For the next two centuries, the Egyptians revolted again and again. Each time, the Persians cruelly squelched the rebellion.

Cambyses II captures Pharaoh Psamtik III.[76]

What Happened When Alexander the Great Showed Up?

In 334 BCE, Alexander the Great marched into Asia with a massive coalition army of Macedonians and Greeks. He fought his way from Turkey to Gaza. However, the Egyptians welcomed him with open arms. They had detested Persian rule. The priests crowned Alexander as their new pharaoh.

Alexander built the gleaming new city of Alexandria at the mouth of the Nile. Its blend of Egyptian and Hellenistic (Greek) culture made it the ancient world's center of scientific and mathematical breakthroughs. When Alexander unexpectedly died at only thirty-two, his generals divided up his enormous three-continent empire. The Macedonian General Ptolemy took Egypt. His descendants ruled as pharaohs for three centuries in ancient Egypt's final dynasty.

Who Was the Last Pharaoh and How Did She Die?

Cleopatra VII was the last pharaoh of Egypt. When her father died in 51 BCE, she became pharaoh with her thirteen-year-old brother and husband, Ptolemy XIII. The two hated each other. Rome was on the brink of morphing into an empire and wanted Egypt. When Julius Caesar arrived in Egypt, Cleopatra joined forces with him against her brother, who died in the war. Cleopatra and Julius Caesar became lovers and had a son together named Caesarion. The relationship ended abruptly when Rome's senators stabbed Caesar to death in 44 BCE.

Cleopatra had been in Italy with Caesar but fled back to Egypt after his assassination. A few years later, Rome's new rising star, Mark Antony, met Cleopatra and fell under her spell. Rome's consul, Octavian (who became Caesar Augustus), was Antony's great rival. He went to war against Antony and Cleopatra, and the lovers lost and committed suicide in 30 BCE. At this point, Egypt became a province of the Roman Empire.

Cleopatra with her son Caesarion as a cupid[77]

What Is Ancient Egypt's Legacy?

Where do we start? Ancient Egypt continued to influence art, religion, and culture for millennia. They made revolutionary advancements in mathematics, science, and medicine that influenced Greek scholars in the days to come.

The Egyptians gave us the pyramids and obelisks, massive architecture that demanded advanced skills in quarrying and construction. They promoted harmony throughout society.

The ancient Egyptians developed irrigation systems that enabled them to produce bumper harvests and provide grain to the Roman Empire for centuries.

The ancient Egyptians took other civilizations' technology, like the chariot, to new heights. While the Middle East used heavy clay tablets to send letters or record data or literature, Egypt developed papyrus, an early type of paper. The hieroglyphics they wrote on that paper inspired the Proto-Sinaitic script, the ancestor of the alphabet we use today.

Roundup Activity: Multiple Choice

Underline the correct answer. Check your answers in the back of the book.

1. Who was the most famous pharaoh of the Nineteenth Dynasty?
    a. Amenhotep III
    b. Hatshepsut
    c. Ramesses II
    d. Tutankhamun
2. Who attacked Egypt but was defeated by Ramesses III?
    a. The Babylonians
    b. The Greeks
    c. The Hittites
    d. The Sea Peoples
3. What Persian king used cats as a secret weapon?
    a. Cambyses II
    b. Cyrus the Great
    c. Darius the Great
    d. Xerxes I
4. Who ruled Egypt after Alexander the Great died?
    a. The Libyans
    b. The Macedonian General Ptolemy and his descendants
    c. The Persians
    d. The Romans
5. Who was the last pharaoh of ancient Egypt before it fell to Rome?
    a. Cleopatra VII
    b. Hatshepsut
    c. Ramesses II
    d. King Tutankhamun

Answer Key: Roundup Activities

Chapter 1: Who Am I?

1. Dedi	I was the first king of a unified Egypt. A hippo killed me. **(6. Narmer)**
2. Djoser	I was King Narmer's wife. After he died, I ruled Egypt until my son grew up. **(7. Queen Neithhotep)**
3. Imhotep	I built Egypt's first pyramid and rescued Egypt from a famine. **(2. Djoser)**
4. Khnum	I was the god of the Nile. I got angry when my temple fell into disrepair. **(4. Khnum)**
5. Khufu	I was Djoser's right-hand man. I was also an architect and priest of the sun god Ra. **(3. Imhotep)**
6. Narmer	I was a Fourth Dynasty king who built three pyramids until I finally got it right. **(9. Sneferu)**
7. Queen Neithhotep	I built Egypt's Great Pyramid, the highest in the world. **(5. Khufu)**
8. Rededjet	I was a magician who could reattach an animal's head that had been cut off. **(1. Dedi)**

| 9. Sneferu | I gave birth to triplets. One baby was Userkaf, first king of the Fifth Dynasty. **(8. Rededjet)** |

Chapter 2: What Happened When?

1. Ahmose begins the New Kingdom and the Eighteenth Dynasty. **(8)**
2. Ahmose conquered the Hyksos once and for all. **(9)**
3. Amenemhat I usurped the throne and started the Twelfth Dynasty. **(2)**
4. Mentuhotep II united Egypt again, beginning the Middle Kingdom. **(1)**
5. Seqenenre was killed, and Kamose became king. **(7)**
6. Sobekneferu, the "Beautiful Crocodile," died. **(3)**
7. The Egyptians regrouped and formed the Sixteenth Dynasty. **(5)**
8. The Hyksos conquered Memphis. **(4)**
9. The Seventeenth Dynasty replaced the Sixteenth Dynasty at Thebes. **(6)**

Chapter 3: Fill in the Blank

The ancient Egyptian's favorite drink was **beer**, which they liked to drink through a straw. Because of the heat, they liked wearing lightweight clothing made from **linen**, which the ladies wove from flax. A scribe had to attend school for **twelve** years to learn all the hieroglyphic symbols. The Egyptians believed **Amun** was the creator of the universe. Egyptian artists used **proportion** to indicate the most important person in the painting or sculpture. The Egyptians thought the scarab beetle's dung ball represented the **world**.

Chapter 5: Pop Quiz

1. Who was the goddess of fertility and motherhood? **(Taweret)**
2. What did the ancient Egyptians believe happened to the ka part of the soul after death? **(They thought it stayed in or near the dead body.)**
3. What was the role of the king in ancient Egyptian religion? **(The king was the mediator between his people and the gods.)**

4. Why did the Egyptians consider Isis to be the "mother of the pharaohs"? **(She was the mother of Horus, and the Egyptians thought their pharaoh was the earthly representation of Horus.)**
5. What god weighed the hearts of dead people? **(Anubis)**
6. Who was the god of the sun and one of the most important deities in ancient Egyptian religion? **(Ra or Amun-Ra)**
7. How did Osiris become the god of the underworld? **(His brother Set killed him and chopped him into pieces. His wife Isis put him back together but couldn't keep him alive, so he became the god of the dead.)**
8. Why did the ancient Egyptians bury the shabtis dolls with a dead person? **(They thought these dolls became people who did the work for them in the afterlife.)**
9. What was the purpose of the Book of the Dead? **(It had magic spells and instructions for the journey to Duat.)**
10. What ceremony was held just before placing a mummy in its tomb? **(The Opening of the Mouth)**

Chapter 6: Crossword
Who or where?

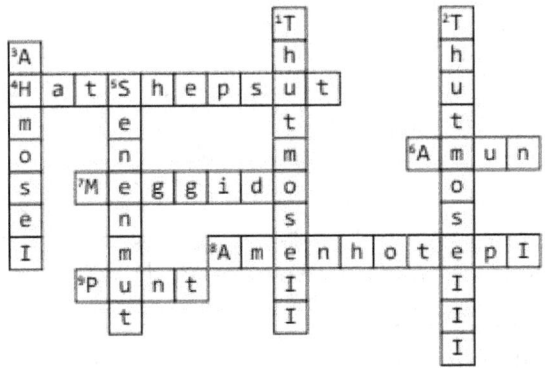

Across
4. I co-ruled with Thutmose III
6. I was a god. Hatshepsut said I was her father
7. Where Thutmose II won his 1st great victory
8. My astronomer invented the water clock
9. Hatshepsut sent an expedition here

Down
1. I married Hatshepsut when she was 12
2. I co-ruled with Hatshepsut until she died
3. I chased the Hyksos out of Egypt
5. I was Hatshepshut's Chief Minister & architect

Chapter 7: Two Truths and a Lie

- Akhenaten promoted the worship of the moon god.

Chapter 8: Word Search

A	N	K	H	E	S	E	N	A	M	U	N	
M	A	I	A								O	
E											V	
N	E	T	A	N	E	H	K	A			R	
H	O	R	E	M	H	E	B				A	
O											N	
T											R	
E	R	A	K	H	K	N	E	M	S		A	
P					Y						C	
I				I								
I			T							Y		
I	S	U	P	P	I	L	U	L	I	U	M	A

1. I was King Tut's grandfather (Amenhotep III)
2. I was King Tut's grandmother (Tiye)
3. I was Tut's father, the religious revolutionary (Akhenaten)
4. I was Tut's wet nurse and tutor (Maia)
5. Neferneferuaten and I ruled Egypt just before King Tut (Smenkhkare)
6. This was my new name after King Tut and I got married (Ankhesenamun)
7. I was King Tut's regent and the pharaoh after him (Ay)

8. I was the Hittite king who died of the plague after capturing Egyptian soldiers (Suppiluliuma)
9. I became king after Ay and erased King Tut and his father from the records (Horemheb)
10. I was the lord who financed Howard Carter's discovery of Tut's tomb (Carnarvon)

Chapter 10: Multiple Choice

1. Who was the most famous pharaoh of the Nineteenth Dynasty?
    c. Ramesses II
2. Who attacked Egypt but was defeated by Ramesses III?
    d. The Sea Peoples
3. What Persian king used cats as a secret weapon?
    a. Cambyses II
4. Who ruled Egypt after Alexander the Great died?
    b. The Macedonian General Ptolemy and his descendants
5. Who was the last pharaoh of ancient Egypt before it fell to Rome?
    a. Cleopatra VII

Here's another book by Enthralling History that you might like

Free limited time bonus

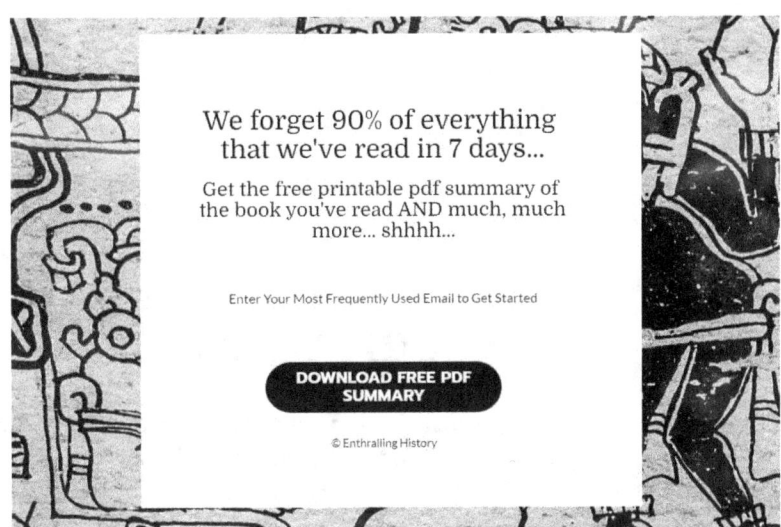

Stop for a moment. We have a free bonus set up for you. The problem is this: we forget 90% of everything that we read after 7 days. Crazy fact, right? Here's the solution: we've created a printable, 1-page pdf summary for this book that you're reading now. All you have to do to get your free pdf summary is to go to the following website: https://livetolearn.lpages.co/enthrallinghistory/

Or, Scan the QR code!

Once you do, it will be intuitive. Enjoy, and thank you!

Bibliography

Agence France-Presse. "New Quest Aims to Settle Debate over Which River Is Longest – Amazon or Nile." *Voice of America*, June 27, 2023. https://www.voanews.com/a/new-quest-aims-to-settle-debate-over-which-river-is-longest-amazon-or-nile-/7154329.html.

"Ahmose, Son of Ebana. "The Expulsion of the Hyksos," San Jose State University. Accessed February 17, 2025. *https://www.sjsu.edu/people/d.mesher/hum1a/Lecture-2-Egypt-Reading.pdf.*

Arnold, Dorothea. "Image and Identity: Egypt's Eastern Neighbors, East Delta People, and the Hyksos." In *The Second Intermediate Period (Thirteenth-Seventeenth Dynasties). Current Research, Future Prospects*, edited by Marcel Marée. Leuven: Peeters, 2010.

Bietak, Manfred. "From Where Came the Hyksos and Where Did They Go?" In *The Second Intermediate Period (Thirteenth - Seventeenth Dynasties): Current Research, Future Prospects*, edited by Marcel Marée. Leuven: Peeters, 2010. https://www.academia.edu/10074987/_From_where_came_the_Hyksos_and_where_did_they_go_in_M_Mar%C3%A9e_ed_The_Second_Intermediate_Period_Thirteenth_Seventeenth_Dynasties_Current_Research_Future_Prospects_OLA_192_Leuven_2010_Peeters_139_181.

"Byblos," Articles on Ancient History, Livius.org, updated November 9, 2020. https://www.livius.org/articles/place/byblos/.

Enmarch, Roland. "Some Literary Aspects of the Kamose Inscriptions." *The Journal of Egyptian Archaeology* 99 (2013): 253–63. http://www.jstor.org/stable/24644936.

Eusebius. *Egyptian Chronicle*. Translated by Robert Bedrosian. Robert Bedrosian, 2008. http://www.attalus.org/armenian/euseb.html.

Gardiner, Sir Alan H. *Egypt of the Pharaohs.* Oxford University Press, 1979.

Goncalves, Isabelle. "Exploiting and Crossing the Egyptian Eastern Desert during the Pharaonic Era." In *Networked Spaces,* edited by Caroline Durand, Julie Marchand, Bérangère Redon, and Pierre Schneider. MOM Éditions, 2022. https://doi.org/10.4000/books.momeditions.16431.

Hernández, Roberto A. Díaz. "The Role of the War Chariot in the Formation of the Egyptian Empire in the Early 18th Dynasty." *Studien Zur Altägyptischen Kultur* 43 (2014): 109-22. http://www.jstor.org/stable/44160271.

Josephus, Flavius. *Of the Antiquity of the Jews Against Apion: Book One.* The University of Chicago. Accessed February 17, 2025. https://penelope.uchicago.edu/josephus/apion-1.html.

Kamrin, Janice. "The Procession of "Asiatics" at Beni Hasan." *The Metropolitan Museum of Art Symposia: Cultures in Contact from Mesopotamia to the Mediterranean in the Second Millennium,* edited by Joan Aruz, Sarah B. Graff, and Yelena Rakic. Yale University Press, 2013. https://www.academia.edu/30529730/The_Procession_of_Asiatics_at_Beni_Hasan_in_Cultures_in_Contact?auto=download.

Levy, Thomas E, Edwin C. M. van den Brink, Yuval Goren, and David Alon. "New Light on King Narmer and the Protodynastic Egyptian Presence in Canaan." *The Biblical Archaeologist* 58, no. 1 (March 1995): 26-35. https://doi.org/10.2307/3210465.

Lundström, Peter. "The king lists of Africanus." Pharaoh.se. Accessed February 17, 2025. https://pharaoh.se/africanus-king-list.

Morenz, Ludwig D. and Lutz Popko. "The Second Intermediate Period and the New Kingdom." In *A Companion to Ancient Egypt: Vol. I,* edited by Alan B. Lloyd. Wiley-Blackwell, 2010.

Redford, Donald B. "Egypt and Western Asia in the Old Kingdom." *Journal of the American Research Center in Egypt* 23 (1986): 125-43. https://doi.org/10.2307/40001094.

Ryholt, Kim. "The Turin King-List." *Ägypten und Levante / Egypt and the Levant* 14 (2004): 135-55. http://www.jstor.org/stable/23788139.

Shaw, Garry J. "The Death of King Seqenenre Tao." *Journal of the American Research Center in Egypt* 45 (2009): 159-76. http://www.jstor.org/stable/25735452.

Shortland, Andrew J., ed. *The Social Context of Technological Change: Egypt and the Near East, 1650-1150 BC.* Oxbow Books, 2016.

Silverman, David P., Josef W. Wegner, and Jennifer Houser Wegner. *Akhenaten and Tutankhamun: Revolution and Restoration.* University of Pennsylvania Museum of Archaeology and Anthropology, 2006.

"Who Built the Pyramids?" NOVA, 1997.

https://www.pbs.org/wgbh/nova/pyramid/explore/builders.html.

Wiener, Malcolm H. "Egypt & Time." *Ägypten und Levante / Egypt and the Levant* 16 (2006): 325-39. http://www.jstor.org/stable/23790293.

You, Jia. "Origin of Mummies Pushed Back 1500 Years: Study on Embalming in Ancient Graves 'Rewrites' Chapter in Egyptian History." *Science*, August 13, 2014. https://www.science.org/content/article/origin-mummies-pushed-back-1500-years.

Image Sources

1 Created by author
2 Jeff Dahl, CC BY-SA 4.0 <https://creativecommons.org/licenses/by-sa/4.0>, via Wikimedia Commons: https://commons.wikimedia.org/wiki/File:Ancient_Egypt_map-en.svg
3 Jeff Dahl, CC BY-SA 4.0 <https://creativecommons.org/licenses/by-sa/4.0>, via Wikimedia Commons: https://commons.wikimedia.org/wiki/File:Khnum.svg
4 https://commons.wikimedia.org/wiki/File:Design_of_the_Abydos_token_glyphs_dated_to_3400-3200_BCE.jpg
5 Photo zoomed in. Quibell,1898, pl. 13, CC BY-SA 4.0 <https://creativecommons.org/licenses/by-sa/4.0>, via Wikimedia Commons: https://commons.wikimedia.org/wiki/File:Narmer_Palette_recto.svg
6 Photo zoomed in. Quibell,1898, pl. 13, CC BY-SA 4.0 <https://creativecommons.org/licenses/by-sa/4.0>, via Wikimedia Commons: https://commons.wikimedia.org/wiki/File:Narmer_Palette_verso.svg
7 Captmondo, GFDL <http://www.gnu.org/copyleft/fdl.html>, via Wikimedia Commons; https://commons.wikimedia.org/wiki/File:MacGregor_Plate_(with_background).jpg
8 Mastaba.jpg: Unknown. Originally uploaded by Oesermaatra0069 at 2006-03-12.derivative work: Master Uegly, CC BY-SA 3.0 <http://creativecommons.org/licenses/by-sa/3.0/>, via Wikimedia Commons: https://commons.wikimedia.org/wiki/File:Mastaba_schematics.svg
9 Charles J. Sharp, CC BY-SA 3.0 <https://creativecommons.org/licenses/by-sa/3.0>, via Wikimedia Commons: https://commons.wikimedia.org/wiki/File:Saqqara_pyramid_ver_2.jpg
10 Photo zoomed in. lienyuan lee, CC BY 3.0

<https://creativecommons.org/licenses/by/3.0>, via Wikimedia Commons: https://commons.wikimedia.org/wiki/File:Bent_Pyramid_%E6%9B%B2%E6%8A%98%E9%87%91%E5%AD%97%E5%A1%94_-_panoramio.jpg

11 Iry-Hor, CC BY-SA 3.0 <https://creativecommons.org/licenses/by-sa/3.0>, via Wikimedia Commons: https://commons.wikimedia.org/wiki/File:Mentuhotep_Closeup.jpg

12 Photo Modified: zoomed in, labels added. Ancient_Egypt_map-en.svg: Jeff Dahlderivative work: MinisterForBadTimes, CC BY-SA 3.0 <https://creativecommons.org/licenses/by-sa/3.0>, via Wikimedia Commons: https://commons.wikimedia.org/wiki/File:Lower_Egypt-en.png

13 Photo zoomed in. NebMaatRa, CC BY-SA 3.0 <http://creativecommons.org/licenses/by-sa/3.0/>, via Wikimedia Commons: https://commons.wikimedia.org/wiki/File:Drawing_of_the_procession_of_the_Aamu_group_tomb_of_Khnumhotep_II_at_Beni_Hassan.jpg

14 Rozemarijn vanL, CC BY-SA 4.0 <https://creativecommons.org/licenses/by-sa/4.0>, via Wikimedia Commons; https://commons.wikimedia.org/wiki/File:Proto-sinaitic-phoenician-latin-alphabet.jpg

15 https://commons.wikimedia.org/wiki/File:Lepsi_Hyks.JPG

16 Metropolitan Museum of Art, CC0, via Wikimedia Commons: https://commons.wikimedia.org/wiki/File:Standing_Hippopotamus_MET_DP248993.jpg

17 https://commons.wikimedia.org/wiki/File:Pharaoh_Ahmose_I_slaying_a_Hyksos_(axe_of_Ahmose_I,_from_the_Treasure_of_Queen_Aahhotep_II)_Colorized_per_source.jpg

18 Photo zoomed in. https://commons.wikimedia.org/wiki/File:Beni_Hassan_(Lepsius,_BH_3)_04.jpg

19 Vassil, CC0, via Wikimedia Commons: https://commons.wikimedia.org/wiki/File:St%C3%A8le_Mercenaire_syrien_18%C3%A8me_dynastie_Neues_Museum_image_%C3%A9claircie_et_perspective_corrig%C3%A9e.jpg

20 https://commons.wikimedia.org/wiki/File:Egyptian_lute_players_001.jpg

21 Jon BodsworthZerida at en.wikipedia, Copyrighted free use, via Wikimedia Commons: https://commons.wikimedia.org/wiki/File:EgyptianScribe.jpg

22 Photo zoomed in. https://commons.wikimedia.org/wiki/File:Egyptian_harvest.jpg

23 Jeff Dahl, CC BY-SA 4.0 <https://creativecommons.org/licenses/by-sa/4.0>, via Wikimedia Commons: https://commons.wikimedia.org/wiki/File:Mut.svg

24 Brooklyn Museum, CC BY-SA 2.0 <https://creativecommons.org/licenses/by-sa/2.0>, via Wikimedia Commons: https://commons.wikimedia.org/wiki/File:Dynasty_12_Egyptian_model_boat_(Amenemhet_I).jpg

25 Boston Museum of Fine Arts, CC BY-SA 4.0

<https://creativecommons.org/licenses/by-sa/4.0>, via Wikimedia Commons: https://commons.wikimedia.org/wiki/File:Nefu_and_his_wife,_official_at_5th_dynasty,_Giza,_Old_Kingdom,_ancient_Egypt.jpg

26 Metropolitan Museum of Art, CC0, via Wikimedia Commons: https://commons.wikimedia.org/wiki/File:Scarab_finger_rign_with_the_name_of_Maatkare_MET_25.3.193_EGDP021780.jpg

27 Metropolitan Museum of Art, CC0, via Wikimedia Commons: https://commons.wikimedia.org/wiki/File:Scarab_finger_rign_with_the_name_of_Maatkare_MET_25.3.193_EGDP021779.jpg

28 Photo zoomed in. Olaf Tausch, CC BY 3.0 <https://creativecommons.org/licenses/by/3.0>, via Wikimedia Commons: https://commons.wikimedia.org/wiki/File:Giseh_Sonnenbarke_07.jpg

29 Althiphika, CC BY-SA 3.0 <https://creativecommons.org/licenses/by-sa/3.0>, via Wikimedia Commons: https://commons.wikimedia.org/wiki/File:Other_ramps1b.svg

30 Photo zoomed in. Walkerssk, CC0, via Wikimedia Commons: https://commons.wikimedia.org/wiki/File:Pyramids_in_Giza_-_Egypt.jpg

31 Eternal Space, CC BY-SA 4.0 <https://creativecommons.org/licenses/by-sa/4.0>, via Wikimedia Commons: https://commons.wikimedia.org/wiki/File:Ba-bird.png

32 Petar Milošević, CC BY-SA 4.0 <https://creativecommons.org/licenses/by-sa/4.0>, via Wikimedia Commons: https://commons.wikimedia.org/wiki/File:Great_Sphinx_of_Giza_(%D8%A3%D8%A8%D9%88_%D8%A7%D9%84%D9%87%D9%88%D9%84).jpg.

33 kairoinfo4u, CC BY-SA 2.0 <https://creativecommons.org/licenses/by-sa/2.0>, via Wikimedia Commons: https://commons.wikimedia.org/wiki/File:Column_of_Akhmenu_Hall_(Luxor).jpg

34 Diego Delso, CC BY-SA 4.0 <https://creativecommons.org/licenses/by-sa/4.0>, via Wikimedia Commons: https://commons.wikimedia.org/wiki/File:Templo_de_Luxor,_Luxor,_Egipto,_2022-04-01,_DD_02.jpg

35 Jeff Dahl, CC BY-SA 4.0 <https://creativecommons.org/licenses/by-sa/4.0>, via Wikimedia Commons: https://commons.wikimedia.org/wiki/File:Taweret.svg

36 Metropolitan Museum of Art, CC0, via Wikimedia Commons: https://commons.wikimedia.org/wiki/File:The_King_with_Isis,_Tomb_of_Haremhab_MET_DP276167.jpg

37 https://commons.wikimedia.org/wiki/File:BD_Hunefer_cropped_1.jpg

38 https://commons.wikimedia.org/wiki/File:Apep_1.jpg

39 Photo zoomed in. Metropolitan Museum of Art, CC0, via Wikimedia Commons: https://commons.wikimedia.org/wiki/File:The_Singer_of_Amun_Nany%27s_Funerary_Papyrus_MET_DT11633.jpg

40 https://commons.wikimedia.org/wiki/File:Anubis_attending_the_mummy_of_Sennedjem.jpg

41 Photo zoomed in. https://commons.wikimedia.org/wiki/File:Opening_of_the_mouth_ceremony.jpg

42 Osama Shukir Muhammed Amin FRCP(Glasg), CC BY-SA 4.0 <https://creativecommons.org/licenses/by-sa/4.0>, via Wikimedia Commons: https://commons.wikimedia.org/wiki/File:Representation_of_the_deified_Amenhotep_I._From_Tomb_TT359_at_Deir_el-Medina,_Egypt._Neues_Museum,_Berlin.jpg

43 Paul James Cowie (Pjamescowie), CC BY 2.0 <https://creativecommons.org/licenses/by/2.0>, via Wikimedia Commons: https://commons.wikimedia.org/wiki/File:Thutmose_I,_copy_of_relief,_Deir_el-Bahari_(MMA_30.4.137).jpg

44 Metropolitan Museum of Art, CC0, via Wikimedia Commons: https://commons.wikimedia.org/wiki/File:Head_of_an_Osiride_Statue_of_Hatshepsut_MET_21II_FIG3A3_1R1.jpg

45 Metropolitan Museum of Art, CC0, via Wikimedia Commons: https://commons.wikimedia.org/wiki/File:Large_Kneeling_Statue_of_Hatshepsut_MET_21V_CAT092R3.jpg

46 British Museum, CC BY-SA 3.0 <http://creativecommons.org/licenses/by-sa/3.0/>, via Wikimedia Commons: https://commons.wikimedia.org/wiki/File:BlockStatueOfSenenmutAndNeferura-LeftProfile-BritishMuseum-August19-08.jpg

47 Charlie Phillips, CC BY 2.0 <https://creativecommons.org/licenses/by/2.0>, via Wikimedia Commons: https://commons.wikimedia.org/wiki/File:Deserted_temple_of_Hatshepsut,_Deir_El_Bahri,_Egypt.jpg

48 Metropolitan Museum of Art, CC0, via Wikimedia Commons: https://commons.wikimedia.org/wiki/File:Upper_part_of_a_statue_of_Thutmose_III_MET_07.230.3_10.jpg

49 https://crosswordlabs.com/view/who-or-where

50 https://commons.wikimedia.org/wiki/File:Menphtah_II_(Merneptah),_figlio_e_successore_di_Ramses_III_(Ramesses_II),_sta_dinnanzi_a_Phr%C3%AA_(Ra)-_due_figure_gigantesche_scolpite_e_dipinte_nell%27ingresso_della_tomba_di_quel_re_a_(NYPL_b14291206-425610).jpg

51 https://commons.wikimedia.org/wiki/File:Amenhotep_II_Uraeus.jpg

52 Jon Bodsworth, Copyrighted free use, via Wikimedia Commons: https://commons.wikimedia.org/wiki/File:Akhenaten_statue.jpg

53 Keith Schengili-Roberts, CC BY-SA 3.0 <http://creativecommons.org/licenses/by-sa/3.0/>, via Wikimedia Commons:

https://commons.wikimedia.org/wiki/File:ReliefFragmentOfAkhenatenWithSunDiskOfAten.png

54 Photo zoomed in. Olaf Tausch, CC BY 3.0 <https://creativecommons.org/licenses/by/3.0>, via Wikimedia Commons: https://commons.wikimedia.org/wiki/File:Luxor_Museum_Statuenkopf_Echnaton_01.jpg

55 Philip Pikart, CC BY-SA 3.0 <https://creativecommons.org/licenses/by-sa/3.0>, via Wikimedia Commons: https://commons.wikimedia.org/wiki/File:Nofretete_Neues_Museum.jpg

56 https://commons.wikimedia.org/wiki/File:Maia_and_tut.gif

57 Jean-Pierre Dalbéra from Paris, France, CC BY 2.0 <https://creativecommons.org/licenses/by/2.0>, via Wikimedia Commons: https://commons.wikimedia.org/wiki/File:Couple_royal_dans_un_jardin_(Neues_Museum,_Berlin)_(11545827426).jpg

58 Djehouty, CC BY-SA 4.0 <https://creativecommons.org/licenses/by-sa/4.0>, via Wikimedia Commons: https://commons.wikimedia.org/wiki/File:Respaldo_del_trono_de_oro_de_Tutankam%C3%B3n.jpg

59 Jean-Pierre Dalbéra, CC BY 2.0 <https://creativecommons.org/licenses/by/2.0>, via Wikimedia Commons: https://commons.wikimedia.org/wiki/File:T%C3%AAte_de_Tout%C3%A2nkhamon_enfant_(mus%C3%A9e_du_Caire_Egypte).jpg

60 https://commons.wikimedia.org/wiki/File:Tutankhamun_tomb_photographs_4_326.jpg

61 EditorfromMars, CC BY-SA 4.0 <https://creativecommons.org/licenses/by-sa/4.0>, via Wikimedia Commons: https://commons.wikimedia.org/wiki/File:King_Tut_over_enemies,_18th_dynasty,_Cairo_Museum.jpg

62 : https://commons.wikimedia.org/wiki/File:Opening_of_the_Mouth_-_Tutankhamun_and_Aja-2.jpg

63 Credit: Dosseman, CC BY-SA 4.0 <https://creativecommons.org/licenses/by-sa/4.0>, via Wikimedia Commons; https://commons.wikimedia.org/wiki/File:Antakya_Archaeological_Museum_Statue_of_Suppiluliuma_sept_2019_5792.jpg

64 en:User:MykReeve, CC BY-SA 3.0 <http://creativecommons.org/licenses/by-sa/3.0/>, via Wikimedia Commons: https://commons.wikimedia.org/wiki/File:Tutanchamun_Maske.jpg

65 ddenisen (D. Denisenkov), CC BY-SA 2.0 <https://creativecommons.org/licenses/by-sa/2.0>, via Wikimedia Commons: https://commons.wikimedia.org/wiki/File:Ushabti_of_Tutankhamun_(KV62).jpg

66 https://commons.wikimedia.org/wiki/File:Ramses_III_(Ramses_II)_lanciato

_col_suo_carro,_e_seguito_da_tre_figli_ugualmente_sul_carro,_assale_una_fortezza_piantata_sopra_una_rupe,_saettandone_gli_atterriti_difensori_(NYPL_b14291206-425634).jpg:

67 Osama Shukir Muhammed Amin FRCP(Glasg), CC BY-SA 4.0 <https://creativecommons.org/licenses/by-sa/4.0>, via Wikimedia Commons: https://commons.wikimedia.org/wiki/File:Pharaoh_Seti_I,_detail_of_a_wall_painting_from_the_Tomb_of_Seti_I_at_the_Valley_of_the_Kings,_Western_Thebes,_Egypt._Neues_Museum.jpg

68 Pbuergler, CC BY-SA 3.0 <https://creativecommons.org/licenses/by-sa/3.0>, via Wikimedia Commons: https://commons.wikimedia.org/wiki/File:Ramses_II_British_Museum.jpg

69 https://commons.wikimedia.org/wiki/File:Tavole_che_ritraggono_il_partimento_inferiore_della_medesima_tavola_87,_fin_dove_comincia_la_battaglia_dei_carri-_(le_tre_ultime_colorate)_(NYPL_b14291206-425654).jpg

70 Photo modified: zoomed in, labels added. O.Mustafin, CC0, via Wikimedia Commons: https://commons.wikimedia.org/wiki/File:F_Crescent.png

71 https://commons.wikimedia.org/wiki/File:Hittite_Chariot.jpg

72 Photo zoomed in. https://commons.wikimedia.org/wiki/File:Tavole_che_ritraggono_il_partimento_inferiore_della_medesima_tavola_87,_fin_dove_comincia_la_battaglia_dei_carri-_(le_tre_ultime_colorate)_(NYPL_b14291206-425654).jpg

73 https://commons.wikimedia.org/wiki/File:Modern_loose_interpretation_at_the_The_Pharaonic_Village_in_Cairo_of_a_Battle_scene_from_the_Great_Kadesh_reliefs_of_Ramses_II_on_the_Walls_of_the_Ramesseum.jpg

74 https://commons.wikimedia.org/wiki/File:Penmaat_Priest_Book_of_the_Dead.jpg

75 Émile Prisse d'Avennes (1807-1879), CC BY 4.0 <https://creativecommons.org/licenses/by/4.0>, via Wikimedia Commons: https://commons.wikimedia.org/wiki/File:Queen_Tausret_%C3%89mile_Prisse_d%27Avennes.jpg

76 https://commons.wikimedia.org/wiki/File:Cambyses_II_capturing_Psamtik_III.png

77 https://commons.wikimedia.org/wiki/File:Venus_and_Cupid_from_the_House_of_Marcus_Fabius_Rufus_at_Pompeii,_most_likely_a_depiction_of_Cleopatra_VII_(2).jpg

www.ingramcontent.com/pod-product-compliance
Lightning Source LLC
Chambersburg PA
CBHW072104050526
44107CB00099B/494